"When Jason walks across that stage on graduation day, a list of people will be there, not to take credit, but to celebrate and shake the hand of the one person who was responsible enough to be there for Jason every day—Jason, himself."

JIM JOHNSTON
Counselor, Cornell Prep High School

Jason: Ward of the State
MARY J. PETERSON

AMP&RSAND, INC.
Chicago, IL

Copyright 2007 by Mary J. Peterson

All rights reserved. No part of this book may be reproduced in any form or by any electronic or mechanical means, including information storage and retrieval systems, without permission in writing from the publisher, except by a reviewer who may quote brief passages in a review.

ISBN 978-0-9761235-5-2

All names and places in this story are fictitious except that of Mary J. Peterson and William E. Peterson.

Design: David Robson, Robson Design

Published by
Ampersand, Inc.
1050 N. State Street
Chicago, IL 60610

Printed in the United States of America

Acknowledgments

Were it not for two very special people, this story could not have been written. Jason and his brother, Kevin, have blessed my life and given me the strength, love and confidence to share our experiences with others.

To my devoted husband, William, thank you for blessing my life with love, support and beautiful memories.

My friend and co-worker, Sandra Walker, who passed away in January 2005, made contributions to this story for which I will forever be grateful.

Thank you to Judith G. Smith for her passionate commitment to my story; to my friend, Ruth Wooldridge, whose encouragement and support never wavered; to Charlotte Russell for many acts of kindness; to my long-time friend, Doris Archibald, for excellent feedback; to my best friend, Christine Steele, for being just a phone call away; and to James Moore for having faith in my ability to write and being willing to listen to endless readings of the manuscript.

Thanks also to my writing instructor, Barbara Croft, at the University of Chicago Graham School, for positive feedback and constructive criticism; to John Robbins and Irene Freelain for teaching me how to use a computer; and to those who graciously gave their time to read early versions of my story and provide vital suggestions and useful comments: Vernita Cole, Ann Dixon, Marsha Frank, Elaine Lieberman, Becka Robbins, Gwendolyn Rogers, Winifred (Winnie) Scott, Gail Wirtz and Doris Zollar.

Most especially, thanks and love to my sister, Leslie and her husband, Norman, for being a constant source of love and encouragement; to my niece, Tia and her husband, Asa, for their enthusiasm and caring spirit; and to my parents, whose love and memory I cherish.

Finally, I thank my editor and publisher, Suzanne T. Isaacs, for embracing my story. Her guidance has been invaluable to me. And thank you to David Robson for his artistic sensitivity and design of this book.

Those who helped me along the way, but whose names are not listed here, also have my sincere appreciation and thanks.

Mary J. Peterson
March 2007
Chicago, IL

Dedication

For Anton. This is your story, too.

In memory of my husband,
Judge William E. Peterson.

"Success is to be measured not so much
by the position that one has reached in life
as by the obstacles which one has overcome."
BOOKER T. WASHINGTON

Call to Action

My journey with Jason has taken very demanding as well as very delicate turns. I have seen Jason and other wards of the state face situations that no child should have to endure. It was my good fortune that Jason accepted my guidance and willingness to bring some level of normalcy to his life. From the start, I wanted him to acquire the tools of education so that he could make better choices. His decision to stay in school when it would have been so easy to drop out is perhaps why I supported his independence and determination to live his life the best way he could within the "System."

There are countless children like Jason in need of hope, love, affection and a measure of stability in their lives. My life is richer and more meaningful because of my relationship with Jason and his brother, Kevin. I hope my story will encourage others to become actively engaged with young people, helping them to develop into positive and productive adults.

Here are some ways to begin with children who are right in your backyard.

Become a Mentor. A strong relationship can help a child who might otherwise be vulnerable to unemployment, homelessness and poverty as an adult.

Become a Respite Parent. If full-time parenting is not for you, you can apply to help foster parents by caring for their adopted children when the foster parents need a break.

Become a Foster Parent. Each state's rules and regulations differ. If full-time parenting is a possibility for you, contact your local department of children and family services.

Become a CASA Volunteer. In this role, you would assist in court cases, seeing to it that children get the services they need.

Become a Contributor. Scholarships, on-the-job training, transportation, supplies are always needed.

To find out more, visit these sites:
www.adoptuskids.org—National adoption website
www.adoptionsunlimitedinc.org—Adoptions Unlimited, Inc.
www.acf.hhs.gov—Administration for Children and Families of the U. S. Department of Health & Human Services
www.nfpainc.org—National Foster Parent Association
www.fostercaremonth.org—National Foster Care Month

Together, we have the power and potential to change the world, one child at a time.

Mary J. Peterson

Contents

- v   Acknowledgments
- vii   Dedication
- x   Call to Action
- 1   A Small, Neglected Child
- 3   Jason's Father
- 6   The First to Listen
- 7   Something Was Lost
- 8   Jason's Mother
- 11   Book Bags
- 12   Happy Birthday
- 14   Life Would Never Be the Same
- 16   Staying Connected
- 21   Wards of the State
- 22   Big Rooms, Little Souls
- 24   Jason's Brother
- 26   Courtroom Experience
- 30   Possessions
- 32   Sharing Their World
- 32   Weekend Visits
- 33   Permission from the Court
- 36   Our First Thanksgiving
- 38   A Delicate Balance
- 44   They Come to Orlando
- 47   Vulnerabilities
- 50   A New School
- 54   Obstacles
- 56   College Admission
- 57   Graduation
- 59   Suddenly, William Dies
- 63   Jason Leaves the Home
- 67   A Happy Surprise
- 70   Jason's Neighborhood
- 74   Lucky Summer Break
- 77   Junior Year
- 80   Steve
- 89   Another Lucky Break
- 96   Steve Dies
- 102   Jason's Senior Year
- 106   Becoming a Legal Guardian
- 109   Jason Comes Home
- 113   Lincoln High
- 117   Jason's Story
- 122   Jason's Day
- 126   Jason Graduates
- 128   College
- 128   "The Life and Times of Jason"
- 130   Epilogue

Jason: Ward of the State

A Small, Neglected Child

In September 1989 when I walked into my classroom at the Lawson Elementary School in Chicago, Illinois, I never thought or even dreamed that one day I would write a story about one of my first grade students. As a teacher, I was trained to impart knowledge through lessons and guide by precept or example. I felt prepared to develop the learning potential of my pupils through drill, discipline and instruction. But I was not prepared for one little boy to touch my heart and soul and change my life completely.

A few years later, after I had retired, a teacher friend called to share some news. During our conversation, she asked about this child whom we had gotten to know so very well. Sarah refreshed my memory about things that I had done for him, noting that on several occasions I had purchased clothes for him. Helping any child in need of clothing would be on my list of things to do or get. But I had never needed to do this for any other student.

As we talked, I recalled one particular incident. I had dashed out after fifteen minutes of lunch duty, gotten into my car and driven across town to the nearest Goodwill store. I knew what this little boy needed—a jacket, sweaters, hats, gloves—anything that would keep him warm during the chilly fall and cold days of early winter. I had told him to wait after class was dismissed because I had something to give him. I didn't know how he was going to respond to my gesture. I thought he might feel embarrassed. But he accepted the plastic bag filled with clothing, smiled and hurried out the door. My voice trailed after him, shouting, "Don't forget to study your sight words and do your homework." That is how the story began.

And here is how it unfolded:

While traveling home from school that afternoon, I thought about how this boy's family might respond to the bag of clothes. I was reassured the very next day. He was seated at his desk, busy with the morning assignment which I'd written on the chalk board. He was wearing a beige and brown sweater from the bag I'd given him. Later that morning when the children went outdoors during recess, he wore the hat I had purchased for him the day before. The bag of clothes had been accepted.

That little boy's name is Jason. Thinking about him as a first grader conjured up a vivid picture of particular sensitivity and need. I knew that most teachers had their special "pet" students—the ones who get to pass out the papers, the ones who are your messengers, the ones you can count on to follow your instructions. You just seem to know who they are right at the beginning of the school year. Jason was not one of those students.

On Jason's first day in my first grade class I saw a boy who was drooling on his paper, barely knowing how to hold a pencil. That first impression of him still makes me shudder. I felt a slight tinge of sympathy. I could see that he needed better care than he was getting. He wasn't dressed properly. He definitely wasn't ready for first grade from appearances of his school work. His work was wet from steady drooling and his desk was messy. Jason would glance around the room with a quizzical look on his face, his eyes darting to and fro, trying to connect with one student or another. He seemed to be trying to secure his place in the class by sending out little bursts of sunshine. He made me aware of his presence. I could see that he was searching for acceptance, but also that he wanted to learn.

Throughout the day, Jason would raise his hand. Each time, I patiently acknowledge him and invited him up to my desk. He was full of questions. I would give each question a substantial answer, and he would return to his seat somewhat satisfied. Then a few seconds later, that small, thin little hand would be up again, frantically waving for another invitation to approach my desk. I didn't think that he was vying for attention, but rather that he was showing his eagerness to know more.

It doesn't sound like it, but Jason was shy and timid—even frail by average standards, almost willowy. I realized early on that Jason was intelligent; however, he needed more time and attention than the average student. It was evident that his school work was not being reinforced at home. Jason's eyes were bright and eager, but from time to time, a gray cloud would push its way to the surface. Many years would pass before I would learn about what was actually going on in Jason's home at that time. He didn't appear poor as in needy, but poor as in neglected. It saddened me that behind that toothy grin was a small, helpless child. In no time at all, he was finding his way into my heart.

Jason's Father

It was time for parents to come to school for the concluding assessment of their child's work and to pick up the final report card. There was much preparation for this event. Bulletin boards had to be arranged with brightly colored pictures, graded papers and charts. Folders of work and final report cards had to be prepared. The school was bustling with activity.

This was an important day. Most parents would feel happy and proud of their child's success and accomplishments. But others would be told that their child was not ready for promotion and should repeat first grade. Parents do not want to hear such news. Many feel that it reflects badly on their parenting. I felt that it was a bad reflection of my teaching, but I believed then and still believe today that retaining children in first grade is often a necessary and good thing. My thinking was that if I didn't teach them to read, who would? I didn't want to leave something so vital to their future to chance, and I didn't want to pass that responsibility on to the next teacher.

It wasn't easy to fail a student. Certain guidelines had to be followed. Records had to be kept, notes had to be sent home, follow-up meetings had to be scheduled, test scores and grades had to be available and extra help had to be given to the child. Samples of the student's work had to be kept to present to parents. And without the principal's approval and parents' permission, a child could not be retained no matter how poorly that child performed.

Too often, a child who cannot read becomes an academic and discipline problem or winds up in a special education class or, in the worst case, becomes a drop out. Children like Jason, who had entered first grade with no basic readiness skills, spent the whole year catching up while others were moving forward.

Jason was definitely one of my candidates for retention, but I wondered if his parents would show up. Then, toward the end of the day, Jason's father appeared in my doorway. It was almost time to leave. He said, "Hello, Mrs. Peterson. I'm Jason's father, Mr. Jefferson."

I walked over to greet him, extending my hand in welcome. I said how happy I was to meet someone from Jason's family. One of his parents had finally come.

Mr. Jefferson appeared guarded as I walked him over to Jason's desk. A folder and report card were on top. When he opened Jason's report card, I tried to soften the blow. "Mr. Jefferson, Jason hasn't done well in school this year. You can see from his report card that he is failing. He has struggled all year with reading and math. He has made some progress in mastering the material we've covered, but not enough for promotion to second grade."

The words stung like a bee. Mr. Jefferson slumped over awkwardly, shifting his weight from one foot to the other, and said "Jason is not doing well in school?" I said, "Yes, that's right." Mr. Jefferson just stood there, painfully aware

Jason: Ward of the State

of Jason's grades and lack of progress. In uncomfortable silence I showed him the evidence. I told him that if Jason were my son, I would want him to have success in school and not struggle as he had this school year. Mr. Jefferson looked as if the weight of the world had fallen onto his shoulders and they drooped even lower. "I don't know what to say," he sighed. I remember wondering at that moment why no one from Jason's family had shown any interest in his school work earlier in the year.

In slow, unsteady steps, Mr. Jefferson moved away from me. He just stood there, obviously in deep thought. I broke the tension. "Mr. Jefferson, I would like to have Jason in my classroom one more year so that I can help him do better." I felt sure about my decision to fail Jason, but uneasy about what would happen next.

Mr. Jefferson forced a faint smile and picked up his son's folder and report card. He glanced at me with the same sorrowful eyes that Jason had, saying, "Nice to meet you, Mrs. Peterson." He walked out and I went home that evening with a heavy load in my heart.

The next morning I found a note under my door. I opened it hesitantly. Inside was a message from Jason's father, short and sweet, right to the point. "Dear Mrs. Peterson, You have my permission to fail Jason." I wondered why he had not offered to help Jason or provide insight as to why he had failed first grade. I felt empty. Thoughts about teaching and making difficult decisions that could affect a child's life were on my mind. I didn't want to see Jason and other children who needed more help become lost in the system.

What was left of the school year passed quickly. There was a steady flow of teaching and testing and grading papers and discussing progress with parents. School ended in June and the children were more than ready for summer vacation. We discussed summer plans. Several hands were raised. I heard all about what would be happening that summer. I glanced over at Jason. He was fidgeting with something in his desk. The happy plans the children were sharing didn't seem to affect him in the least. I didn't ask Jason how he would be spending his summer vacation. He appeared lost and defeated. I worried that perhaps I had not done the right thing by failing him, but deep down I knew I had to help him master those basic skills. I was happy that he would be in my classroom for one more year. I was hoping that I would be able to reach him better next time. But I still had a sinking feeling, and it wouldn't go away, no matter how hard I tried to ignore it.

The First to Listen

The new school term filled me with anticipation and excitement. "I must double my efforts," I thought. On the first day of school most students were clean and neatly dressed—but not Jason. He sat there in a faded, worn out blue shirt and torn pants. The pants were too short, "flooding" as the students would say. I tried not to focus on his poor appearance. My hope was that his parents would take better care of him this year, but that hope faded as each day passed. I asked many times, "Where are your supplies, Jason?" and "Jason, did you do your homework?" His look stopped me in my tracks. His eyes were empty and pleading. I decided to buy the supplies he would need to do well in school. My mission was to help him advance to second grade.

During Jason's second year in first grade I gave a creative writing assignment. This exercise was designed to encourage the children to express their feelings. The subject was "If I Had One Wish."

My classroom was located on the first floor and led to the playground. The weather that day was delightful, so I took my class outside where they could read their stories to one another in the warm, fresh air.

Generally, the students volunteered to read, but this day I decided to call upon them. When Jason walked to the front of the class he seemed uneasy about the sea of faces watching him. He stammered a bit at first, but then began his story.

I was surprised that he did not write about "If I Had One Wish." Instead, he wrote, "Mrs. Peterson is the first person ever to listen to me. She hears what I am saying." The warm air now seemed still and hot. You could hear a pin drop. The entire class was listening intently. He went on to say, "I never had anybody listen to me like she does." My eyes were welling with tears. I was deeply moved. I had no idea that I had made such an impact on this young boy. His classmates were very respectful and appeared touched by Jason's story. They clapped enthusiastically when he finished and their eyes followed as he walked back to his place. They showed a new level of respect for him, and I did, too, even though I was completely caught off guard by what he had to say.

Other students read their stories, but I couldn't stop thinking of Jason's. I wasn't prepared for the degree to which his simple words stirred my innermost soul. "I was the first person to listen to him." In all of my years of teaching, this moment was one that I came to treasure most. Years would pass before I would get a glimpse into those aspects of Jason's life that would make his statement so incredibly remarkable.

Something Was Lost

The community surrounding our school was very inviting. Most of the homes were sturdy, brick bungalows. There were two or three flat apartment buildings, too. Some homes were octagon shaped with concrete steps and banisters, others were Georgians and others were large frame houses. Trees lined the streets and yards were well kept. Seasonal flowers were in bloom everywhere. In the springtime the ground was prepared for the summer gardens. In the fall colorful leaves covered the trees. Neighbors greeted each other cordially.

I parked my car in front of a church located near the school. It was a mighty structure of brick and stone. Solid wooden doors and brass handles were polished to perfection. The stained glass windows gleamed. I loved those beautiful windows. The tall steeple anchored the community. It was a real pillar of strength and lent a feeling of calm and tranquility. This was not a community in decline. It bustled with activity. Men were dressed in business suits or uniforms. Women dressed modestly and children were well groomed. There was a real sense of belonging and beauty. In my memory, it was ideal.

The children were a mirror of this community, except for Jason. He stood out from the rest. For reasons that I did not yet know, Jason and the surrounding neighborhood were not a perfect fit. Something was missing, something was lost.

Jason's Mother

During Jason's second year in first grade there was a marked improvement in his abilities, attitude and self-confidence. He would raise his hand on occasion, but mostly he was answering questions, not steadily asking them.

I don't remember why, but one day I took a picture of him raising that eager little hand. Maybe I wanted to etch that into a lasting memory. Maybe I wanted to capture a scene of innocence and enlightenment. Maybe I wanted to freeze the sight of a bud beginning to bloom. Whatever the reason, Jason was becoming my true testament to teaching and learning as well.

That school year passed rather quickly. It was time for parents to pick up the final report card. It took a lot of work

Jason: Ward of the State

to prepare my classroom for parent visitations. It was orderly. All the books were arranged neatly on the shelves and current work was posted on the bulletin boards.

I took note of all the parents who had attended the first report card pick-up and those who had not. Jason's parents had not come the first time, so I didn't expect to see them at the end. But I had miscalculated. This time, Jason's mother came. I was pleasantly surprised to see her. "Hello, may I help you?" I asked as she entered my classroom.

"I am Jason's mother and I came to get his report card."

"Come right in. I am so glad to have the chance to meet you. I am Mrs. Peterson." I offered her a seat in the front of the room, next to my desk. She was hesitant at first. She surveyed the room then looked at me with a slightly drawn mouth and fixed gaze. She seemed a little afraid. I tried to appear as friendly as I could so she would be comfortable.

"How is Jason doing in school?" she asked.

"I've seen much more progress this year," I replied, trying to speak directly to her, but she was looking down, nervously moving her hands in her lap. A slow, steady grin began to gather at the corner of her mouth.

Then Jason appeared and stood at his mother's side, waiting to hear what I would say next. "Jason has told me about you." I waited for her to say more.

"Jason is really learning at a steady rate," I said. Mrs. Jefferson looked at me, her face totally blank. I wanted to know more, to understand what kept Jason's parents away from school.

I spoke slowly. I surely did not want to scare her away on the first visit. "You should be very proud of your son," I said, waiting for a reaction. I didn't get one. I related further that Jason was reading much better, his vocabulary skills had improved, he was doing his homework and the quality of his penmanship had soared. From the corner of my eye I could see Jason beaming. I opened my grade book and related several passing marks that Jason had received in phonics, language arts and spelling. I talked about what was expected of him and how he had accomplished the goals. Mrs. Jefferson looked interested but distant.

Jason's mother had an attractive face, but she was pale and appeared sickly. She was light skinned like Jason and her hair was sandy brown with amber highlights. It wasn't arranged in any particular style. She avoided eye contact and, with arms folded protectively against her chest, spoke in a hushed tone that was barely audible. She smiled at Jason's accomplishments but didn't appear to be overjoyed at his academic progress.

Mrs. Jefferson arose from the chair and stood in front of me, rather stoically, as I continued to speak highly of Jason, his good grades and all of his efforts. I was thrilled to relate this information to her, knowing that most parents love to hear anything positive about their child. Her reaction puzzled me. She looked up with an empty expression as I reviewed his standardized achievement test results in reading and math. I closed the grade book, handed her Jason's report card and asked if she had any questions. She frowned a little but did not say a word.

Grinning from ear to ear and with great pride, Jason walked his mother over to his desk. She stood there and scanned the folder but made no comment. With a faint smile she whispered "oh" several times. Jason was standing close to his mother, as if to guard his papers and protect her at the same time. He was passing, moving forward on his own path, headed for second grade. I was very proud of his progress.

Book Bags

When Jason started second grade I purchased a book bag, filled it with school supplies and gave it to him. I did the same when he entered third grade and fourth. A book bag symbolized school and had within it all the materials he would need to do his work. Pencils, pens, papers, erasers, glue, folders and other items that he would need to be successful in school were in the bag. My joy, pride, anticipation and an incentive to do well were also enclosed.

Why did I purchase book bags for Jason but not for any of my other students? Most students came prepared for school, but Jason never had what he needed to succeed. For me, a book bag signals a level of interest and readiness. A child who does not have materials and supplies is at a disadvantage from the start. I did not want Jason to fall behind because he did not have the right supplies. I thought of the crayons, paper, pencils and pens as silent soldiers, waiting to march with Jason towards the next assignment. He eagerly accepted the book bag with its new supplies and that made me feel good.

One of my favorite sayings is, "A carpenter wouldn't go to work without his tools; therefore, students shouldn't come to school without their book bags."

For Jason, I wanted book bags to be synonymous with school and achievement at all times, including feelings of hope and expectation. When I bought a book bag for Jason, I was showing concern and caring, and my wish for him to do well in school. It was also a way to stay connected. Each year as I placed a new book bag in his hand, I silently communicated that education is an attainable goal.

Happy Birthday

In April 1993, when Jason was in fourth grade, he told me that he was having a birthday. Naturally, I asked him the date. It wasn't weeks away, as I had anticipated, but the next day. It wasn't unusual for children to share their birthday celebrations with teachers and classmates. However, Jason wasn't as enthusiastic about sharing this important news as other children were. He was in a somber mood. The expression on his face came nowhere near the happiness and exuberance most children feel on this occasion. He was sad, his eyes were downcast.

Oftentimes, parents would send cupcakes, cookies or soft drinks to school, giving the entire class a reason to celebrate. But for Jason, this was a day without sunshine. I didn't recognize the signs and symptoms, but I knew that something was wrong.

Every school day was filled. There wasn't time or energy to delve deeply into the personal lives of my students. That was the role of school social workers, psychologists and nurses. They had leverage to support and serve youngsters with particular pains and problems. I thought that they should address Jason's concerns. Someone had to be there for a child like him. There was an invisible line that separated my personal and professional lives, but I had crossed that line many times when I thought someone had to take an active role in the life of a troubled student. Often, I became the caring adult in a child's life.

Questions about Jason would pop in and out of my head at school and at home. How could such a young, sweet child be filled with grief? What could possibly be happening in his life to spoil his childhood? What could be tormenting him? Why was he so anguished? It really disturbed me that Jason was despondent.

His birthday presented an opportunity to bring some joy into his life. I decided to purchase something new just for him. I pictured Jason's face upon receiving my gift. I could see a sad frown turn upwards into a wide, open grin.

I went to the children's clothing store on my way home from school. There I found rack upon rack of children's clothes in bright colors, shapes and sizes. I sifted through different patterns and textures and settled on a blue slack set. I'm not sure why I chose the color blue. Maybe he had suggested blue. Maybe he had used the color in one of his pictures. Maybe he wore blue more than any other color. Blue certainly was the color of the sky and I could envision blue skies in his future.

I was smiling from the inside out. I held my purchase tightly under my arm, not wanting to lose the excitement and energy that the gift held. I wanted this small gift to lift Jason's gloom.

At the end of the next day, which was the last before spring break, my class was busy. Students were leaning over their desks searching for papers and books. Some children were cleaning off the tops of their desks and others sat quietly, waiting for the dismissal bell to ring. Over the hustle and bustle, I explained the homework assignments that were due upon their return to school and gave the final instructions for the day.

Throughout the process, I was thinking about Jason. I sent a messenger to his classroom with instructions for him to stop by my class before leaving school. I did not want the rest of the children to see me giving him a gift.

I was eager to present his birthday surprise and waited anxiously. When Jason entered my room, I was seated at my desk. His eyes lit up like a Christmas tree when I said "Happy Birthday!" and gave him the brightly colored package. The worried, solemn look melted into a wide grin. He carefully packed the present deep down into his book bag. "Thank you," he said, and hurried out the door. He could hear my voice trailing after him, "Don't forget to do your homework!"

I couldn't contain the big wide smile across my face either. How could buying a gift for Jason bring me so much joy and contentment? I wanted to capture that moment forever. When I played the scene over in my mind, it always warmed my heart to know that I had brought a bit of blue sky into a little boy's cloudy life.

Life Would Never Be the Same

My husband and I were going to Orlando, Florida over the spring break to soak up the sun and relax. We were set to leave the evening of the last day of school and there was plenty to do. My husband, who was a lawyer, had gone downtown earlier that Friday to submit some documents to the courts before going to the airport.

I had asked him to stop and pick up sheet music I had ordered for a song titled "Trees." The children had read the story "The Pine Tree" in which a little tree struggles to stay alive when nature itself seems to be working against it. They loved the story and wanted to put on the play. Just before spring break, I had begun to gather props, songs and other materials for the play. My husband was always supportive and I could always rely on him to help my school efforts.

He picked up the sheet music and then hurried home so we could take care of a few last minute details. I was so glad that our luggage had been packed the day before. We ate a snack before heading out. Instead of taking the shuttle bus as we usually did, William signaled a taxi and we rode in comfort to the airport. Little did I know that within hours, my life and the world as I knew it would change dramatically.

We arrived at the airport with plenty of time before departure. William bought a newspaper and read portions of it to pass the time. We walked outside to see the new monorail trains in front of the airport. A cool breeze of sweet spring air brushed lightly across our faces.

Jason: Ward of the State

We returned to the terminal and went to our gate immediately. This was before 9/11 so the extra security measures we have today weren't a factor. We boarded the plane, crowded with spring break vacationers and took our seats. It was a pleasant ride. Both of us were tired and happy to be able to spend the entire week in Florida.

We arrived in Orlando at about 10:00 p.m. I gathered our carry-on baggage and began to exit the plane. On the way down the aisle, I noticed that something was terribly wrong with William. His speech had become slurred to the point of incoherent. His mouth was drooping to one side. Every step he took was extremely difficult. The flight attendant also noticed that he was having trouble and rushed to his side. William wasn't responding to our inquiries about how he was feeling. My heart was beating so fast, but I knew I had to stay calm and rational. We got him into a wheel chair and an ambulance was called. I'm sure William was as startled and concerned as I was about what was happening to his body, but he couldn't respond. He was rushed to the nearest hospital. The flashing lights and sirens numbed my senses even further. I was in shock. What had happened? One minute William was fine and well. In a split second he needed emergency treatment. My heart was pounding. A whirlwind of activity surrounded us.

At the hospital, William was wheeled into the emergency room. I spent the following minutes and hours in a state of extreme anxiety and confusion. The doctor finally came over to speak with me and said that William had suffered a stroke. At the time I did not know anyone—friend or family member—who had had a stroke, so I had no point of reference. I had seen the devastating effect of a stroke on the body, but I didn't know what caused it.

This life altering episode was overwhelming at first, but I learned about the condition and what to expect during the recuperation process. I had to accept that life would never be the same. In a matter of minutes, William had gone from a strong, vigorous, completely independent person who had gained stature in life and had traveled the world extensively, to being dependent and confined. I had to learn to care for him and nurse him back to health. That was my main priority.

William was hospitalized for months in Orlando. I had to adjust to living in a different city, learn more about his medical needs, and prepare for his recuperation back in Chicago. I had to plan my life according to his needs. I decided not to go back to teaching and retired. I didn't realize at the time that I was closing one door and opening another. I didn't have time to go back to school and explain this life changing event to my class and that disturbed me at first, but my heart and home belonged to William.

Caring for William was all consuming. My day was totally scheduled around his physical, medical and emotional needs, but I thought about Jason frequently.

After returning to Chicago, I spoke often with my friend, Sarah. She would give me updates about things happening at school and over the next two years, she delivered book bags to Jason for me, playing an integral and vital role in bridging the gap and allowing me to stay connected to him.

Staying Connected

The two years since William's stroke passed quickly. At home, I rarely had a minute to think about school but in the back of my mind, I often wondered how Jason was faring. It was now the fall of 1995 and Jason was starting sixth grade. I became anxious about buying a book bag for him. It gave me so much pleasure to help prepare him for a new school term. I always took extra time to choose the best book bag. The stores were full of school clothes, notebook paper, pens, pencils, folders and, of course, new book bags. There was a huge range of colors and styles but that special book bag for Jason somehow had to stand out from the rest. In my mind it was my job, and mine alone, to find that treasured book bag so that Jason could have a solid start in school like all the other children.

I had very fond memories of buying and sending book bags to Jason. Then it happened. A phone call from Sarah on a Sunday evening changed everything.

I recognized Sarah's voice right away, but I could sense that something was different. Usually, I called her when I was ready to send the book bag, but on this particular day, she called me. We exchanged pleasantries then Sarah related news and updates about some of the students and teachers at school. That was followed by silence. I wondered what could possibly be wrong.

Finally she spoke and I could hear worry and agitation in her voice. I took a deep breath not knowing what to expect. Then she said, "I have something important to tell you. Jason is no longer at the school." My heart dropped. I wasn't prepared for such news, though it should not have surprised me because children transfer in and out of schools every day. However, this was not what I wanted to hear. Now I didn't know where Jason was.

I was upset and speechless. I imagined Jason out there somewhere not properly prepared for school, needing that book bag. A role I truly relished had vanished into thin air. How was I to stay connected? How could I still play an active role in Jason's life? I needed to give him his book bag. What would I do without this ritual?

Until now, I had not realized how much that book bag meant to me.

Finally I calmed down, gathered my senses and tried rationalizing that maybe it was time to let go. Maybe, I thought, it was time to let his parents buy his school supplies. This notion didn't make me feel any better. Jason wasn't just a former student of mine; he had become a special student. How could someone spoil our bond? How could someone snatch Jason away from me?

I asked Sarah to check around the neighborhood to find out where the family had gone. Sarah sensed my fear and frustration. She was my friend and she took the time to ask parents and people in the community if they knew anything about where Jason was and what school he was attending. I was in desperate need of any information whatsoever. I wanted know how Jason was doing.

Finally, after a period that seemed to last forever, Sarah located Jason's family. I listened intently so as not to miss any details. She told me that Jason was living with a relative way across town, on the west side of Chicago. She had gotten a phone number. I wrote it down. I was so relieved. I couldn't contain my joy at finally knowing where he could be reached.

Periodically, I checked my purse to make sure the paper with Jason's phone number on it was still there. This number was my only link to Jason and his family. Even though I had the phone number, I didn't try to reach him right away because I didn't know what to expect. He was now living with relatives. I wondered if they really were his relatives and if they were taking good care of him. Would they welcome me with open arms or shun me for showing an interest in him?

After a few weeks, I decided to make that call and request a visit. His relatives responded politely. I hoped that I hadn't sounded too desperate. True, I had been his teacher, yet the person on the other end of the phone sensed that I had become much more. My unsteady voice echoed my urgency and need for information. I was eager to see him again and I hoped he was as eager to see me. In my heart, I knew that I was making a difference in his life, but tiny bits of doubt and fear had begun to cloud my vision. I spoke with authority, yet I could hear my tone softening with each comment. Something inside me swelled with pride just mentioning his name. If for no other reason I had to deliver his book bag to him. It was my duty. I knew he would be expecting it. And it gave me a purpose for seeing him. No matter what it took, getting Jason's book bag to him became one of the most important tasks in my long list of things to do.

On the day I traveled to the west side to see Jason, my husband decided to accompany me. William must have felt that I really needed his support, but he was also eager to meet this young boy about whom I had spoken so fondly. He shared in my joy at seeing Jason and it showed.

As we drove, I was casing the neighborhoods. How would Jason fare in this new environment? I noticed maple, oak and spruce trees blowing in the distance. Some streets had green lawns and shrubbery, but many had scattered patches of greenery or nothing at all. Some sidewalks were paved but there were many more with open spaces, deep holes, cracks and jagged edges protruding from the ground. Broken bottles littered the lawns. Pop cans and trash were strewn in the streets and alleys. It disturbed me to see this mess but I was even more concerned about Jason's reaction to it. It filled me with disgust that Jason had to live under these conditions. Boys of all ages and sizes were milling around or hanging out on corners, doing nothing but watching every passing car and person. Their fixed stares and empty eyes were not friendly. They surveyed every inch of our car. We were not comfortable riding through the area.

I turned the corner slowly. I hadn't seen Jason since April 1993 when I gave him that birthday present at school. Now it was September 1995, almost two and one-half years later. I wondered how much he had changed during this time and how he was going to react to seeing me under these circumstances.

We approached a large brownstone building with a balcony on the second floor. A few children were hanging over it, as if they were looking for something. The relative must have told Jason about my visit because as our car pulled up to the curb, one of the children began to wave frantically. The other children enthusiastically waved with him. In no time, I found that familiar face. I got out of the car and walked around to the passenger side. I waved to all the children. Jason's face was the only one beaming with excitement. When I saw those familiar bright eyes and toothy grin, I was relieved and very happy.

Jason came down and examined every detail of the car. He surveyed the back and front seats, the tires, the hood, and even the dashboard. He could see that someone new had accompanied me. I introduced them and Jason acknowledged my husband politely. He appeared satisfied and happy when I handed him the book bag. His smile widened then vanished quickly when I said, "Have a good school year and study hard." He said, "I like the book bag. Thank you." Then he turned and ran upstairs to his friends and family on the balcony. They waved and shouted their good-byes over other loud noises in the neighborhood.

I looked back at Jason as we left. I didn't want to say good-bye. I didn't want to leave him. But knowing that I had delivered that book bag gave me a sense of accomplishment.

We drove back home listening to soft music, interrupted only by William remarking, "He seems like a very likable and happy young boy, and his wide grin lit up his face when you handed him the book bag."

It seemed to take an eternity to reach our residence. I parked the car in our usual spot, but my thoughts were on that balcony with Jason. I glanced at William from the corner of my eye and saw a solemn expression on his face. Did his worry and uncertainty mirror mine? I didn't dare ask because I was lost in my own thoughts, not wanting to be found.

Wards of the State

Shortly after our visit, I learned from Jason's aunt that he had become a ward of the state and was living in a group home. I hung up the phone. I was in shock. We had just left him brimming with happiness, and now this? What had happened? What in the world had happened to his family and why couldn't they save him?

All kinds of questions were swimming in my head. Going from childhood to adulthood is daunting enough for any child, but going through life as a ward of the state has to be impossible. I thought about Jason being moved from place to place, with no family, no foundation. I knew I had to be steadfast in my determination to help him.

Time passed slowly. Each day I became more and more bewildered and physically upset about his situation. I was so afraid for him. Just the words "ward of the state" spoke of abandonment and betrayal. I had read so many stories about children in foster care, group homes and institutions. It was difficult not to compare Jason's situation with those I had read about. It was the only frame of reference I had. Would Jason become a drop out or join a gang and not go to college?

Through his aunt, I found out the name and address of the group home where Jason was staying. I immediately called to inquire about him. The person on the other end was reluctant to speak to me, but after a short while, I was able to voice my concerns. "How is Jason doing?" The staff worker said, "He is adjusting." Her answer was certainly to the point, but any information about Jason was music to my ears. I knew then and there that I had to see for myself exactly what was going on. It was becoming difficult to explain my relationship to Jason any further. I had indeed become Jason's mentor, his advocate. That solidified my position in his life.

The staff worker sensed my sincerity and gave me the name and address of the facility where Jason was staying. I thanked her graciously and hung up the phone. For a few minutes, I sat motionless, trying to digest the information I had just received. Now I knew the location of the group home, and acknowledged, too, that Jason was located in a chamber of my heart.

Big Rooms, Little Souls

After a short period, I decided to visit Jason at the group home. The day was sunny and clear as I drove my car out of the garage and proceeded north. Leaves were starting to change colors and trees were laden with clusters of orange, red and gold. But the beauty of the day couldn't sweep away my concerns about seeing Jason and making him a part of my world again.

I took the time to survey the blocks surrounding the group home. Every detail was imprinted in my mind as I drove down the streets — slowly, like a surveyor. I scrutinized the buildings and their surroundings because someone dear to me lived there.

When I arrived at the group home, which was located on the far northwest side of the city, I saw an old mansion-style brick house with a wide, deep winding porch and a steel railing. There were two floors, each supported by two thick columns of brownish, red stone. It was an older structure, but it appeared to be solidly built with quality materials. The spacious porches were separated by a band of stark, white wood. Wide windows and doors led out to the porches. I imagined that in the past those porches were frequented on hot summer days by prim and proper ladies and gentlemen who could be seen sipping tall glasses of lemonade out there on the veranda. Those images quickly vanished, however. This house was now a home for young boys who had no other place to live.

I couldn't see the entrance right away. It was on the side of the building. I wondered when and how this place had

Jason: Ward of the State

become a group home for children. The building itself offered no answers. It just stood there silently, solemnly, at attention.

As I approached the entrance, I heard soft whispers and the jagged conversation of children and adults. There was no joyful laughter or fun and frolic; just busy noise and controlled chatter. A sense of dread enveloped me. If my feelings were so negative, what were the sentiments of the young children living inside?

When I rang the doorbell, I checked my thoughts and emotions at the door and anxiously waited for someone to answer. My heart skipped a beat as I thought about how Jason would react to my visit. How could I make a difference in his life now? What steps must I take to help him feel safe and secure? I only knew that I had to see for myself how he was doing.

When we finally met I couldn't really tell if he was glad to see me or not. He was in a melancholy mood. I tried to find the right words to comfort him, but all I could think of to talk about was school. School was our comfort zone, the reason for our connection.

Out of the corner on my eye, I saw how this huge house had been transformed into living quarters for "wards of the state." It had great big rooms with little bitty souls in them. Several boys were milling around aimlessly in the area where we sat. They were of different ages. I could hear their silent cries for help. I asked Jason if there was anything I could do. He shook his head to say no. I asked him if there was anything he needed and again he shook his head, no. I felt the need to do something, but what? When I asked him if he wanted me to visit again, I saw a slight glimmer of hope in his eyes.

Leaving Jason in this situation was painful. Our time together had passed in a flash. I rose from my seat, told him good-bye and walked toward the door with feet that felt anchored in cement. As I dragged myself to the car, I was searching for something that I could do to help his situation.

Jason's Brother

The following Saturday, I returned to the group home. As I was ushered into the visitor's room, I noticed another young boy in the area where Jason and I were sitting. To my surprise, he turned out to be Jason's brother, Kevin. I started a conversation with him. Kevin was tall and lanky and appeared to be older than Jason, who was 12. As I learned, Kevin was 14 years old and attending high school on the far south side of the city. I could see their brotherly love, as well as the shame they felt about being "wards of the state."

I was filled with a strange, aching feeling as I sat in the living quarters of this massive group home. I scrambled for the right words to say. Odd as it seemed at the time, I began to talk about the importance of getting good grades and going to college. I tried to paint a picture of education being their way out of a desperate situation. However, school was not the first thing on their minds at that time.

While we were talking, a young boy was pleading with someone on the other end of the telephone. "I just want to go home," he said. Then there was silence. The tension in the air was thick as smog.

Kevin and Jason nervously exchanged sideways glances. I was too afraid to look up right away. I felt empty, awkward inside. I thought the boys must have been feeling the same thing. Even though home isn't necessarily the safest place for many children, they still want to be home. I wanted these boys to know that I cared.

Kevin was the vocal one, but even his tongue was tied. Jason was staring straight ahead. Not knowing exactly what to say or how to say it, I merely asked if they would like me to visit again. Both said, "Yes."

The next week I returned and it was during this visit that I decided to help both boys. Given their circumstances and situation, there was no way that I could separate them. They were two birds trapped in a cage, their wings clipped, their spirits dampened. They were the remnants of a family. I was thinking about how these brothers were going to survive the "System" and who would be around to cushion their disappointments and loss. I thought that if I helped them together, they would in turn keep me in their lives. It seemed like the right thing to do.

And so it began. Every weekend I would drive to the group home, pick up Kevin and Jason and take them to the shopping mall where I bought clothes and other things that they wanted. At the top of their list was a large trunk with a lock on it. They intended to keep their things locked up because some of the items that I had gotten for them were stolen by the other kids. I couldn't help feeling sympathy for the loss of their things. Their family and friends had been taken from them and now their personal possessions were being taken as well. Clothes and items can be replaced but how could I possibly replace their sense of loss?

My middle class upbringing had not prepared me for issues like this. I came from a large, loving family. We had many people in our home but the notion of having to lock up possessions was unthinkable to me. I brought this to the attention of the supervisor.

The supervisor informed me that things are often stolen in a group residential home. She also told me that most of the residents had been abandoned by their families and even though stealing was not condoned, it may be their way of stealing love and attention. Her explanation gave me a clearer view of their world. This situation left me feeling sad and empty. In the midst of this difficult period in their lives, I became even more resolved to be their anchor and strength.

Courtroom Experience

During one of my daily phone calls to the group home to inquire about Jason and Kevin, I learned that they were going to be attending a mock trial. It was being sponsored by young members of a local Bar Association. The purpose of their outreach program was to familiarize children in a group home with the operations of the courts and to alleviate some of their fear. The courts were a big part of the lives of these children whether they wanted it or not.

Hearings are frightening enough for adults and the notion of young children having to go to court was chilling. However, I thought that the mock trial would be especially beneficial for Jason and Kevin. It was going to take place on Saturday, at the Dirksen Federal Building downtown. I asked the supervisor if I could attend. I wanted to be there to support the boys in any way I could.

The traffic wasn't heavy as I passed parks, trees, beaches and the beautiful lakefront as I drove to the Dirksen Building. The sky was bright blue and a few billowy clouds were drifting by. I passed children playing and enjoying the weekend off from school. How sad that some children had to attend a mock trial in a federal court building on such a wonderful day.

The weather changed as I walked the three blocks from the parking garage. It had begun to drizzle. That was typical of Chicago weather.

The Dirksen Building was still and solemn. It was an imposing structure made of brown steel and glass. The gray marble floors and dark walls gave the lobby a stark appearance. There weren't many people around because most of the courtrooms were closed.

I went straight to security check. The staff was prompt and professional yet impersonal in checking people in. My belongings were placed on a conveyor belt, I walked through a screening device, and then to the elevator. As I

Jason: Ward of the State

waited I couldn't help thinking that some of the boys might commit major crimes one day. Maybe a few would become repeat offenders with regular court appearances and prison a part of their everyday lives. On the other hand, maybe this mock trial experience would deter them from a life of gangs, drugs and crime. These thoughts made me shudder.

I entered the courtroom and found a seat in the back of the room. I watched as the supervisors got the group settled down and acclimated to their surroundings. These children were getting ready to take part in a courtroom drama and they would have leading roles and responsibilities. The loud bang of the gavel brought the court to order. The children didn't move a muscle when the imposing figure of the judge entered the courtroom. You could tell that the supervisors or someone from the Bar Association had taken time to prepare the boys for this experience. They appeared prompt and ready to go. But I felt sad about the whole thing because I would have preferred seeing these young children enjoying life, playing games and just having fun.

The judge began by explaining that as an officer of the court, he is invested with the authority to administer justice; he is the one who decides upon the merits of persons and things; he is the one who examines, forms opinions and passes judgment on numerous issues, major and minor. Then he put this information into simpler language so that the children could understand. "I make sure that the person gets a fair trial," he explained. I admired the judge for taking extra time to make this situation as painless as possible. I also admired him because the tone in his voice was so reassuring. He was working on a day when the courts weren't in session and he appeared to have the best interests of the children at heart. I thought about how judges see things through the naked eye of the law, and how this judge was making an effort to see the law through the eyes of children.

Next, the role of the prosecutor was defined. He is the one who sues to redress violations of the law. He is a lawyer who represents the state. Kevin had been assigned this job. I could see the subtle changes in his posture as he assumed this real life position. He stood proudly when his name was called and walked with a slow steady gait to the front of the courtroom. With his chest out, his shoulders back, he played this role with authority and conviction. I could see the wheels turning. He was truly thinking.

The function of the defense was presented next. Again, the judge took pains to explain the role. This is the party who opposes and denies the truth, validity, or sufficiency of the plaintiff's complaint. Speaking to the children, he said, "The defense is the person being charged with the crime or offense." He added, "It takes a lot of skill to defend oneself."

This position was given to another child who was almost as tall as Kevin. When his name was called he, too, slipped easily into his role. He demanded attention in his own quiet, subtle way. He straightened up and stood erect before the judge.

The judge then addressed the twelve children who were going to be the jury. I could tell that he was trying to smooth over the stark reality of the courtroom and the special language and terms that would be used. The children slid to the edge of their seats when the judge reiterated their special function and role in this case. A moment later, they marched dutifully to the actual jury box. It didn't take them long to get settled. They were noticeably alert and aware of their surroundings. They cased the front of the courtroom cautiously.

A few minutes later all eyes were fixed on the drama which was unfolding before them. From where I sat, the courtroom took on a whole new dimension when the stage was set and everyone was in place. The mock trial looked like the real McCoy. I was actually amazed at what I was watching. Kevin, the prosecutor spoke first. He presented his case clearly and with conviction. I was so proud of him. The

Jason: Ward of the State

defense also put on a good presentation, stating certain points with force and zeal. The jury was alert and attentive.

Jason had hurt his leg the previous week and was walking with crutches, so he couldn't participate in the mock trial. He never turned around to see who else was in the courtroom. At first I was relieved that he didn't know that I was there. I hadn't told the boys that I would be attending, so they wouldn't have expected to see me. From where I sat, I could tell he was uncomfortable. His body was turned so that his leg was stretched out on the bench. But, because the courtroom had become so important in his own life, he couldn't dismiss what was happening. I caught Jason's expression in a few fleeting glances. There were wrinkles on his forehead and he was squinting. Once or twice, Jason's eyes were darting around the room but never in my direction. He was obviously restless and moved back and forth in his seat, but I thought that he was following every moment of the proceedings.

After the arguments the children were instructed to go back to their seats. The judge spoke to the supervisors briefly then addressed the children saying, "You did a good job today. Remember what you have learned." The children warmed to his statement that they had done a good job.

I remained seated as the children rose to leave. Jason spotted me first and vigorously waved for me to join him. I felt he was surprised yet happy to see me. I asked about his leg and he assured me that it would be okay. Just as Kevin was walking over, I overheard the supervisors directing the children out of the courtroom. I quickly patted Kevin on the shoulder and said, "You really did a great job. You should feel proud of yourself." I looked at the children as they slowly exited the courtroom, marched outside and got on the van to go back to the group home. I watched and waited until they left.

Even though they were given some practice with the procedures and policies of a courtroom, these were still young children, having no choice but to grapple with adult concerns. It was a sad, sad situation.

Possessions

Shortly after I arrived home from my visit to the Dirksen Building, I received a frantic call from Kevin. He and Jason were at the group home. He was anxious and sounded almost desperate. He related an incident that had happened in the van on their way from the court house to the home.

Earlier, when I learned that Jason had hurt his leg and was using crutches, I took a bag of candy and cookies to him to lift his spirits. During their return from the Dirksen Building, another child snatched his bag of goodies. From Kevin's frantic voice I gathered that a small skirmish had ensued and the supervisor took the bag. Both boys were upset about the whole thing.

In a normal situation, small occurrences like this do not require anything other than a discussion and return of the property. But for these boys, each small episode turned into a major conflict. It was if they had to fight viciously for the few belongings they had. Tiny problems were magnified and molehills became mountains at the drop of a hat. It took a great deal more effort and energy than warranted to overcome these "huge" obstacles.

I spoke to Kevin in a steady, calm voice. I said, "These things sometimes happen and if you calm down and speak to the supervisor, things will be straightened out." He didn't hear much of what I was saying. He was still screaming into the phone that the candy had been stolen and the supervisor took it and he didn't know what to do. I tried to allay his fears. He slowly calmed down and handed the phone to Jason. He, too, was overly anxious and angry. I repeated the same words to him in hopes of bringing some resolution to the problem. It was during this conversation that I realized that I was going to be the voice of reason and influence in their lives. They were feeding on my very words.

I thought about how I would feel if something like this had happened to me in their situation. This wasn't about a stolen bag of candy. The candy had been a gift, a personal, small treasure given with love. It was special. I began to understand the strong emotions in both boys.

I took a deep breath then spoke with the supervisor. She listened intently to my concerns and to those of the boys. I'm sure she acted quickly to defuse the incident, but I had to make it clear that these boys needed to have their candy returned and that it was important for them to own what was rightfully theirs. She agreed with me and the candy was returned.

This was a minor hurdle. I felt certain that the impact of the courtroom drama had triggered their over-reaction. How difficult it must be to live in a group home with strangers. How difficult it must be to have to stand over and fight for your few possessions. And how extremely difficult it must be to have to watch and wait for someone else to change your life.

I had been to court for traffic violations but for these two boys the courts were their parents and the state was as a member of the family. I closed my eyes and imagined wrapping them in a protective shield and delivering them safely home. What home? Where would I take them? I had made the commitment to be their anchor. Now I was becoming their life line as well.

Sharing their World

When I picked up the boys to take them shopping, they always wanted to go to Goldblatt's to purchase workmen's clothes—large dark blue shirts and oversized slacks. They looked like prison uniforms to me, but these clothes made the boys happy. We shopped at different stores and looked at different outfits but they always settled on the same things. Taking them on shopping adventures allowed us to share in each other's worlds. Living in a group home limited their experiences of many things. I tried to make life for them as normal as possible, especially when we went shopping and to a restaurant afterwards.

During this period, I gave Kevin one of my husband's old cameras. It occurred to me that precious moments of childhood would be lost if there were no pictures. Kevin had developed an interest in photography. He thought he was ready to focus, aim and shoot. He was selective, only taking pictures that meant something to him. He took pictures of Jason doing various things and making faces, reflecting their brief moments of pleasure. Nevertheless, these pictures did not mask their pain.

Weekend Visits

After a period of time, Jason and Kevin were allowed to visit us on weekends. They would take the "el" train to a downtown station where I would wait for them in my car. More often than not they were over an hour late. Waiting for long stretches of time gave me a chance to reflect. Then I'd see two pairs of eager eyes searching for my car, two young stomachs hungry for food, and two sets of limber legs walking in my direction. While waiting I thought about new places we could discover together. These special adventures were as important to me as they were to them. No matter what I had to do, my main purpose was to share weekends with them on a regular basis.

Thanksgiving was approaching and I couldn't stand the thought of the boys being at the group home for the holidays. I asked if they would I like to spend Thanksgiving Day with my family and they enthusiastically shouted, "Yes!" I was thrilled, but I had to ask their supervisor for permission. She informed me that they had a court date in November and I could formally request a home visit at that time.

Just before the court date, a caseworker came to my home to determine if it was a suitable place for the boys to visit. She asked me if I wanted to know about the boys' case history. This created a dilemma. On the one hand, I did not want to judge or be put in a situation that would cloud my vision or dampen my dreams for the boys. I wanted to be in the center of their world, not on the outside looking in. So I hesitated.

Permission from the Court

The court date was set for about three weeks before Thanksgiving in 1995. I was prepared to tell the judge what I knew about Jason and my request to have him and Kevin celebrate Thanksgiving with my family. I remember the morning of the hearing very clearly. While driving to court I felt a little anxious. I reviewed my statements in my head. I wondered if I was trying too hard. What if I didn't make a good impression with the judge? What if he didn't grant the visit?

While these questions floated in my mind, visions of the two years I had Jason in my first grade classroom flew by. I remembered how sweet and innocent he was. He was so likable and never caused any trouble. A calm, peaceful feeling overcame me and then I knew that any reservations about what I was trying to do were pointless. I felt more at ease with my decision to ask for permission for the brothers to spend Thanksgiving with my family

I arrived at the court building, went through security and was directed to the second floor, to juvenile court. The benches outside the courtroom were filled. I started looking for Jason and Kevin. Finally I spotted them, huddled together, their winter coats buttoned up around their necks. This struck me as strange since they were inside, not outside the building. I walked up and touched Jason lightly on the shoulder. Both looked up and I saw how scared they were. My heart sank. I realized that they didn't fully understand what was going to happen here. I extended my arms to hug them and then we sat in silence, eyes fixed forward and feet frozen to the floor.

Each minute seemed to last an eternity. Finally a caseworker introduced herself and inquired about my relationship to Jason and Kevin. I told her that I had been Jason's first grade teacher and I wanted him and his brother to join my family for Thanksgiving dinner. The caseworker jotted down my name and informed me that when the case was called I should go into the courtroom and wait for instructions. I was a little nervous.

When their case was called, the boys were whisked off into a private room and I entered the courtroom. I found a seat in the back row and surveyed the room. Who were all of these people? In each corner of the room there was a different group of people actively engaged in serious conversations. Some were glancing in the direction of the judge. I was observing the proceedings and was aghast at what happened next.

At this point, I did not know how or why the brothers had been made wards of the state. Nor did I want any information that would taint the special bond we shared. I really wanted to remain neutral and keep the cold hard facts of their lives separate from our relationship.

Jason: Ward of the State

In the course of this proceeding, however, I realized that I was a small, insignificant fish. I listened intently to what the judge was saying, hoping that what I was hearing wasn't true. At first it appeared that the judge was going to grant custody to their mother. Then the judge asked if the mother was present in the courtroom. My heart skipped a beat as two women approached the bench. They were neighbors. They spoke to the judge in hushed tones, relating that the mother was ill and had not been outside the house for a long period of time. Ill? What kind of illness? Why were her children taken from her in the first place? Could they postpone the hearing, allowing time for the mother to get well? I was thinking about how desperately her children needed her. Was the mother reaching out to her children by sending the neighbors? Was she trying to send a message to the court that she loved her children and wanted to be with them?

Then the judge said that the father had not attended any of the previous court hearings either. I wanted to cry. I wanted to shout to the top of the rafters. I didn't want to disrupt the proceedings, but I wanted to be heard. How could I state my intentions? How could I show interest and concern for these children without arousing suspicion? What could I do right now to show that I care?

After a while the judge reviewed the materials at hand, and spoke to the fact that the interests of the brothers would best be served by remaining wards of the state. These words were devastating. I couldn't begin to imagine the impact all of this would have on Jason and Kevin. They were being punished for their parents' neglect. I knew that I had to support them the best way I could.

I thought about an article in the *Sun-Times* newspaper which posed the question, "Where are the dads when kids are in turmoil?" In my mind, fathers should take responsibility for the welfare and protection of their children because it is the right thing to do. "About one-third of America's children grow up without their biological father, and about 40 percent of those children have not seen their father in more than a year." These figures were daunting, and impressive.

In that courtroom I made a vow to disprove all of the negative facts and figures concerning some youths. Jason and Kevin could beat the "System" and succeed and I was going to be there to fight their battles and help them win.

Our First Thanksgiving

I waited for what seemed like an eternity for an answer from the court as to whether or not I could take the boys to my home for Thanksgiving dinner. Every time the phone rang, I jumped and my heart skipped a beat. Sometimes I would answer the phone and listen to the person on the other end without hearing a word that was said. I felt embarrassed that this happened on more than one occasion, but I was waiting to hear about the boys. That was the only call that was important to me and the only one that mattered. A supervisor finally called and said permission had been granted.

Thanksgiving dinner took a lot of planning. This was going to be a special Thanksgiving and I wanted everything to be perfect. My husband shared my enthusiasm. Neither of us could imagine celebrating the holiday without family and friends. I knew that I took family for granted. I was only a phone call away from everyone close and dear to me. It seemed so easy for my husband and me to be surrounded by family during times of triumph or tragedy.

On Thanksgiving morning I drove to the north side to pick up Jason and Kevin. They were clean and neatly dressed and appeared a little apprehensive about meeting my family. I let them know that the evening would be an enjoyable one. The boys looked out the window for most of the trip. When we arrived at the house, I reassured them that my family was friendly and there was no reason to worry about anything.

Jason: Ward of the State

Jason and Kevin sat in the living room as I put the final touches on the dinner. They sat at far ends of the sofa, looking sad and forlorn. There was a wide, empty space between them. I watched them from the kitchen. They looked so small, lost and afraid that it broke my heart. I had to make them feel welcome and at home. I had so much wrapped up in that dinner. I wanted them to leave with good memories and to become part of my family as well.

It is our custom at Thanksgiving to form a large circle, holding hands as my husband says a prayer and others join in with personal poems and praise. My nieces and nephews would jump into the middle of the circle to read hand written poems. Some tributes were short, others were long. But each word, phrase, sentence or verse was music to our ears—a beautiful scene, with everyone joined together hand-in-hand.

My husband asked everyone to bow their heads as he gave a wonderful, long soulful prayer. He tried to send out rays of love and affection in his prayer. The words came easily for him and each tribute was heartfelt. He always made comments about our love for each other and how much family means to us. I was especially proud of the short poems and tributes my nieces and nephews read. We had so much for which to be thankful.

Everyone was making a concerted effort to include the boys in our circle of prayer. They were on either side of me, so I was holding one of their hands. I squeezed tightly and tried to transfer all the love and affection I could through my fingertips. I was praying for them to have peace and stability in their lives, too. A segment of my Thanksgiving prayer was answered immediately. The boys warmed up to the group and I saw a smile on their faces when the last "amen" was said.

When dinner was over and all the guests were gone, the boys helped me clear off the tables and put away the folding chairs. They eagerly volunteered to sweep the floor and help with cleaning the dining room and kitchen. I was quite aware of how polite they had been all day. Obviously, someone had taught them well. They were not rude children.

As I was driving them home later that evening, I saw the first signs of Christmas approaching. Red and green lights lined the tops of buildings downtown.

I told the boys that my husband and I would be leaving in a few weeks for Orlando for several months and I asked if they wanted me to send them anything. Jason asked for magazines about Michael Jordan. He was a diehard Michael Jordan fan. Kevin wanted me to call him every Sunday. So for the next three months, I purchased magazines about Michael Jordan and the Bulls for Jason. I mailed them every Saturday morning so that he would receive them by Wednesday. And I called Kevin every Sunday night. Sometimes I spoke to Jason but not often because he was usually watching the Bulls playing ball on TV. I came to realize that by religiously keeping my promises to the boys, I was weaving a web of trust between us. It was a wonderful feeling.

A Delicate Balance

During the months that we were in Orlando, Jason wasn't doing well in the group home. It appeared that he had problems with authority. In fact, he was having serious conflicts with all of the supervisors except Steve. Jason had to adhere to rules and regulations that were new to him. He also had to deal with the consequences of breaking the rules.

Actually, he had multiple parent substitutes like supervisors, social workers, lawyers and the psychologist. Each one presented a different personality for this little boy to understand, and even more difficult, to trust. It didn't seem fair. His parents were not available for him. These new people were forced into his life—without even asking his permission. I believed that Jason was in trouble with authority because of a lack of trust and stability.

Before my husband and I left for Orlando, Jason had been skipping school and whatever the issues, they weren't being addressed. On one of my daily calls to the group home, the supervisor told me that Jason was having a terribly difficult day. He had not gotten out of bed all day. This news disturbed me.

I asked the supervisor to tell Jason that I was on the phone and wanted to speak with him. I was hoping that he would get up and come downstairs to speak to me. The supervisor placed me on hold. I had my doubts, but then I heard a faint "Hello." "Do you want me to come up there?" I asked. "Yes." "I'll be there shortly."

Obviously, things were not right. It was easier for him to crawl into bed and hide under the blankets than to get up and face the situation. Just maybe it would all go away like a bad dream.

I put aside my plans for the day and drove north. During the trip I began to think about children who go through a divorce and are asked to choose one parent over the other. As bad as that is, it does give the child some say in the matter. But when a child is forced to accept abandonment, having no say in the matter, and his parents are still alive, behavior such as Jason's becomes understandable. I was thinking about how careful I had to be whenever I brought up the touchy and sensitive issue of his mother. I had a suspicion that some of Jason's turmoil had to do with his mother. I anticipated that I would be treading on thin ice, but the topic needed to be brought up.

I could relate to Jason's feelings in some ways. My mother's death rang in my ears long after she had passed away. I grieved for years. I tried to cope the best way I could, but nothing could ease the pain and hurt I felt inside. I had family, relatives and friends to support me but they didn't erase the loss. I could only imagine how it feels when one's mother is alive but the chances of seeing and communicating with her are slim to none. Jason, as with any child his age, needed time to heal and accept what had happened to him.

When I arrived at the group home, Jason was waiting for me in the living room. He looked haggard. His hair was long and tangled. We walked out onto the porch. I asked how was he feeling and he answered okay. I asked how his day had gone so far and again he answered okay. But I knew differently. We stood awhile watching the passing cars. Then I said, "Jason, I know something has been troubling you that we haven't talked about." He gazed off into the distance as I kept right on talking about mothers in general terms. I said, "Mothers are so special. Mothers are so strong, strong enough to bring us into the world. Mothers care about their children and would do anything for them, but sometimes a mother can experience things in her life that weaken her. Sometimes her spirits weaken and she loses hope. She may want things to go a certain way, but sometimes life just doesn't turn out the way she wants it to." Jason could have cut me off at this point but he didn't, so I continued. "I'm sure your mother wants to be with you, but for some reason she can't. That doesn't mean that she doesn't love you. She wants you to be strong. I know sometimes things are hard to understand and deal with, but try to think about what she would want for you. And it's also about what you want for yourself." His eyes would light up then fade away in a flicker. At points he nodded his head, but not often. The dismal look on his face didn't give me much of a clue as to whether I was reaching him. I asked if he wanted to ask me anything. In a crackling voice, with his eyes focused on me, Jason asked, "Why did this have to happen to me?" I didn't have the answer then and to this day, I still don't. I replied, "Sometimes positive things can come from bad experiences," but I really didn't think that was helpful. I changed the subject asking, "Do you want to go to the barber shop to get a hair cut?" He agreed to go. I had to ask permission for Jason to leave the premises. It was granted and we drove away in silence searching for a barber shop. The barber struggled to untangle Jason's hair so that he could cut it. Jason's mood changed a bit and a slight smile emerged as he looked in the mirror, checking out his hair cut.

While we were in Orlando, I called often to check on the boys. It was during one of these phone calls that I learned from a supervisor that Jason's problems with attending school had gotten worse. He wouldn't get out of bed in the mornings and sometimes would stay in bed all day long. I wanted him to go to school and do well in spite of the harsh reality of his situation. The supervisor told me that a special meeting was being called to address this problem. I flew back to Chicago.

I arrived at the group home just before the meeting started. I recognized the social worker and the two supervisors, but not the psychologist and the lawyer. We were gathered in the living room and Jason was there, too, somewhat surprised to see me since he knew I had been in Florida. I was introduced to the group and my relationship was stated. I was a bit nervous but tried not to show any signs of anxiety. I knew I had to be an advocate for him and speak with conviction and purpose. I couldn't dissolve the trust that I had already established with Jason and the staff working with him. As I looked around the room at the professionals seated before me, I became aware that it took all of these people to replace one or both parents. These were strangers making major decisions about Jason. There he sat, listening and waiting for an answer to his problems.

I knew that this meeting was vital to Jason's future. The professionals were sifting through papers with dates and details relating to Jason's actions. Specific behavioral changes, particularly his issues with authority and following directions, were noted and discussed. His school attendance record was reviewed along with his attitude and habits in the group home. I tried to compose myself.

Discussion turned to the possibility that Jason may have to transfer to a more restrictive home downstate because of school absenteeism and problems with authority. This was a major shock. A more restrictive placement would mean stronger rules and regulations. How could that solve the problem? All Jason needed was someone to understand and care for him, support him through these crises. It was mentioned during the meeting that when I called the group home in the mornings, Jason would get up and go to school.

I spoke to the group with as much sincerity as possible about how I always had time to talk to Jason about what was bothering him and about how he needed love and stability, not more restrictions. I even related that I would take him to get his hair cut to boost his morale and build self-confidence and how this was an incentive to attend school the next day. I was willing to help him anyway I could because small favors and attention gave him a reason for living and coping with the situation at hand.

During the meeting, Jason sat with his head down, staring at his hands in silent contemplation. My heart sank to see him so despondent and forlorn. Sending him away to an even more disciplined home would further punish him for things he didn't understand. Jason was hurting so much. I couldn't let him down. I had to be his advocate, a voice of reason.

I cleared my throat and looked directly at the group. I argued that he should stay there at the group home because of the detrimental effects another change would have on him. I said that Jason was only a client and case number to them, but that they needed to acknowledge that he was also a child with hurts as deep as a river and wide as an ocean. I glanced around the room. Jason still had his head down. The educators were contemplating my remarks. I felt overwhelmed yet relieved. I knew that I had given my all to help save him from another drastic change.

Jason: Ward of the State

There was a strange silence. No one spoke right away. The tension could be cut with a knife. A giant wave of uncertainty began to cloud my thinking. I had to stay strong for Jason; I had to stand firm. I glanced at Jason again, still sitting frozen in his chair. He appeared to be sinking in a pool of doubt and fear, and I was there along with him. The meeting seemed to last forever. It was such a critical time for him. When the meeting ended, we exchanged good-byes, I left the room and returned to Orlando.

I felt like a different person traveling back to Florida. There were empty spaces in my heart. I was genuinely sad. I tried to focus on the palm trees, cool waters and beaches, but nothing could divert my attention away from Jason and his dilemma.

Did I make a good enough case on his behalf? Did I speak strongly enough against another placement for him? Did they listen to me with their ears or hearts? I was so dismayed about the situation, I began to wonder if I could really make any difference at all.

Rejoining my husband was difficult. So much had transpired in such a short time. Jason's life was in a delicate balance. One decision could send him away forever and another could leave him in the group home and he could continue to have some contact with me. We tried to keep busy, but Jason lingered in my mind day and night.

A few days later I received a call from Jason's supervisor. She was elated and reported that the parties had taken into account all of the things that I had said. The consensus was to allow him to remain at the group home. I was overjoyed. I could stay actively involved in his life and Jason wouldn't have to adapt to another environment and new people. My husband was pleased by the good news also and glad that Jason had been spared more hardship. We had won a small victory but the war was far from over.

They Come to Orlando

The following year as I was planning our trip to Orlando I told Jason that we would not be in Chicago for the Thanksgiving holiday this year. His face and shoulders dropped to the floor. The sad, solemn look of abandonment that I had seen many times returned with a vengeance. I could barely look him in the face. I knew I had to do something, so I asked Jason if he and Kevin would like to go to Florida with us for the Christmas holiday. He said that he would ask Kevin. Later he told me that they both wanted to go. I was thrilled.

There was so much to do. I did not expect the opposition I would face from the director of the group home. He felt that Jason shouldn't be allowed to go to Orlando because he was not doing much to correct the problems he was having in the group home. I argued once again on his behalf. I said that the trip to Orlando wasn't offered based on his behavior, but as an opportunity to have a nice Christmas. That was all.

It took weeks of calling and talking with staff and supervisors trying to convince the director, who had the final say. These obstacles were new to me and I had to have patience and tenacity. At the end of the second week a supervisor called to say that the director had granted permission.

I always enjoyed watching the store windows change during each season, particularly Christmas. Bright lights were strung around the plump, green trees and the branches were hung with shiny bulbs and ornaments. There was hustle and bustle in the air, candles and wreaths and elves and a big fat Santa Claus. Children were invited to sit on his lap. It was always fun for me.

But this year was different and very special. I had to buy gifts for two boys who were going to spend the holidays with us in Florida. I spent the days leading up to our trip shopping for suitable outfits and items the boys would like. Even though the boys would be traveling to warm weather in Orlando, I shopped for clothing for the cold winter days in Chicago. I bought shirts, pants, socks, and heavy woolen jackets. I purchased colorful large gift bags to place their things in. My spirits soared every time I thought about what I could purchase to make the boys happy. Of course a basketball and school supplies were on my list.

I packed our belongings and prepared for this wonderful holiday. William felt that this was going to be a special time, too. He watched me run errands, make calls and bring home loads of packages. Orlando was a great place to take children because of the many theme parks, rides and adventures. We were looking forward to the trip and to bringing some happiness into the boys' lives.

I regretted the fact that they couldn't travel with us. We had to accept whatever arrangements were made for them. As long as we could be there together, that's all that mattered. William and I had a few days to ourselves in Orlando before the boys arrived. I had put up a Christmas tree and trimmed it with lots of ornaments. Christmas decorations were all around the house. The temperature was in the high 80s.

We went to the airport and waited patiently for our special travelers. I had to sign for them since they were wards of the sate and had left Illinois. The attendant escorted Jason and Kevin off of the plane. We saw two weary, young boys who appeared to be carrying the weight of the world on their shoulders. They held their bulky winter coats close to their chests, apparently fearing that they might be snatched away from them at any minute. The duffel bags swung over their shoulders were bursting at the seams. I welcomed them with open arms and hugs. They cautiously looked around the airport and at all of the people moving swiftly about. They moved hesitantly at first, but with each step they became more and more secure. I told them about all of the activities I had planned for them. I don't remember who was more excited—me or them.

I had told my good friend, Shar, that the boys were going to visit us. She asked if she could accompany us to several of the theme parks. The boys went on all the rides at Disney World and Universal Studios. We spent a day at Wet and Wild, steaming under the blasting sun. We visited Alligator Farm and fed the gators, watching them jump for food. They had a great time go-cart racing. Eating out was just a part of the fun.

Every day we were up and out doing something. It was good the boys had each other because I couldn't go on any of the high rides they enjoyed so much. William joined us when we visited Sea World. He especially wanted to share the Dolphin Show with the boys. It was one of his favorites.

Their personalities completely changed once Kevin and Jason settled into their new surroundings. It was wonderful to see them transformed into happy, energetic boys. It seemed that they had left their cares and worries in Chicago. Now they were cheerful and their wide-eyed expectation was indeed refreshing. Jason's quick wit surfaced. He was the jokester, always coming up with something funny. One day while I was washing the dinner dishes Jason leaned over the counter to tell one of his silly jokes. I thought perhaps it was his way of compensating for his own sad feelings. He enjoyed making other people laugh. He wore a Santa Claus hat around the house, probably because I had asked them to get a hair cut before they left Chicago and Jason's hair was really short. He enjoyed clowning around with that hat. We had many happy moments sitting around the kitchen table with William engaging Jason and Kevin in conversation about where we had gone that day and where we would be going tomorrow.

Christmas Day was the best of all. I had awakened early and had placed the large colorful shopping bags near the Christmas tree. Their names were written in large letters across the front. Christmas music was playing as I prepared coffee and toast for William and me while the boys helped themselves to cold cereal and juice. Presents were opened after breakfast and I had my video camera going. Kevin, of course, being the older brother opened his first. He was grinning from ear to ear. Then Jason opened his gifts—a basketball, and many other wonderful things. I looked over and saw Jason sitting in a chair with his new house shoes on, tapping to the sounds of Christmas music. A bubbly grin was on his face as he continued to entertain us, wearing that goofy Santa Claus hat. Then William began to open his gifts and we all enjoyed sharing in his surprises. In the meantime, my friend and neighbor, Shar, and her husband had come over and brought gifts for Jason and Kevin.

I spent the rest of the morning preparing the remainder of the Christmas dinner. The boys watched sports on TV and played games. We didn't have any ice or snow, but the Christmas spirit was alive and well.

Not once did I see Kevin or Jason go into the refrigerator without asking first. Not once did I see their room messy. Not once did I have to remind them of anything. I couldn't have asked for more polite boys. So when they asked if they could stay a few days longer, I didn't hesitate to say yes. Instead of seven we spent ten days basking in the sunshine of each other's joy. It was a very special Christmas and it will be etched in my memory forever.

Vulnerabilities

After our Orlando trip, I became an even more integral part of the boys' lives. The months turned into years and one memory blended into another. It became evident that Kevin needed even more of my care and attention. He was now in his junior year of high school. My intention at the time was to get Kevin thinking about college. I thought it would inspire and motivate him.

Kevin was basically an independent and self-motivated person. He lived in the group home while attending high school. He would leave very early in the morning and he didn't return until late evening. He would get some food, relax a while and then go to bed only to start again bright and early the next day. He remained after school and hung around with his friends before returning to the group home. Kevin went to school every day, traveling over two hours each way, but he didn't mind. To my knowledge he had not had any serious problems living in the group home for some time. He had accepted my role in his life naturally, without ever questioning my authority or influence.

Kevin was content, or so I thought. Little did I know that he had low expectations. His grades were poor and reflected his lack of focus and concentration on school work. I learned that the school Kevin attended had a tracking system which allowed him to select his curriculum himself and he was on a track that was going nowhere. I knew that Kevin spent time worrying about how he could keep the family intact. He loved his brother and other members of his family. I had to ask myself, does a child ever give up on that idea? Kevin never complained about school. I didn't know he was just barley making the grade.

A turning point came when Kevin sat in on an after school reading class with a friend. The assignment was to read *Jane Eyre*. Kevin wasn't required to purchase the book since he was not assigned to the class. When he told me about this I immediately went out and bought two copies. I had read the novel years ago and remembered key passages and details of how Jane was orphaned and sent to live with her aunt. I needed to refresh my memory by reading it again.

Weeks had passed since I had given Kevin the book. One Sunday afternoon I was preparing dinner for William and the boys when Kevin mentioned *Jane Eyre*. I was thoroughly surprised that he had read ahead of me. We shared page upon page of interesting facts and details. I recalled that education offered Jane the possibility of improving her position in society. I wanted to hammer this idea into Kevin so that he could see the similarities in his own life. Kevin was hooked on this story. Each chapter gave me an opportunity to use examples and compare them to Kevin's situation. It became easier and easier to stress education as we journeyed through the novel together.

During one of our sessions, Kevin revealed that he wasn't interested in college. He said that he wanted to go to a trade school. I was startled at first, but remained calm. Over time, as we had discussed the importance of education as well as the importance of getting good grades, Kevin's thoughts shifted toward college. His grades improved. I suggested tutoring to help with some of his difficult classes and he readily accepted. Every Saturday morning I would drive him across town to a church that offered tutoring. I could see subtle changes in his attitude as time passed. Both boys were vulnerable and in danger of losing their sense of direction and hope. This made me try even harder to keep them focused and grounded in education.

Jason, in the meantime, was struggling in elementary school. He had to attend a school near the group home, which may or may not have met his needs. The school was located in a neighborhood that was ethnically diverse. I secretly hoped this atmosphere would help to round out his experiences by giving him more exposure to other cultures.

Sometimes when I drove under the "el" tracks while going to the group home, I would listen to the thundering trains and say a silent prayer that the boys would be kept safe and out of harm's way. I would hear the loud rumbling of the trains speeding down the track and would hope at the same time that the boys would stay on track and in school. Often I would see police cars lined up in the middle of the street and wonder if one of the boys had encountered problems with the law. There was a gang problem in the area. I truly felt the group home tried to buffer the elements of the streets. But still I worried that Jason, being at a vulnerable age and in an unstable family situation, could fall victim to the gangs who would take over and steer him to a path of destruction.

The gang element was strongly evident everywhere, from the graffiti on the walls of buildings to the groups of aimless boys hanging around the neighborhood with nothing to do but watch and wait for trouble. It bothered me that this might become another hurdle for Jason to cross and overcome.

I joined forces with Jason's teachers to check on his progress in and outside of school. I had to be strong and steadfast in my efforts to help him and divert his attention away from negative influences. Every time I talked to Jason on the telephone, I had to drive home the message: stay in school and keep out of trouble.

Jason was promoted to eighth grade but I thought that his chances of finishing elementary school were dwindling with each passing day. There were many negative forces pulling him in different directions. The gangs offered some children a home or place of belonging and for Jason, a solid family and foundation were missing. It appeared easy to become attracted to gang culture and difficult to circumvent its attraction. It became my main mission to save him from the streets. But how? I didn't know exactly what to do, just that I had to do something.

A New School

It's now September 1997 and the beginning of another school year. Jason is about to enter eighth grade. A few weeks before school was to begin I called Steve, one of the supervisors at the group home, and the one with whom I spoke most frequently. I had given him a list of Catholic schools to be considered for Jason. I figured that a good

Catholic school would provide him with the structure and discipline he needed. I also thought that it would buffer him against the negative activities that were distracting him at his current school. I rationalized that a Catholic school would offer religious beliefs and fundamentals that were sorely missing in his life. It would also remove the dangers he faced when walking to his neighborhood school. If he were going to a Catholic school, he would probably be bussed. I wanted Jason and Steve to visit these schools and select one where Jason would feel comfortable. I really wanted Jason to decide on a Catholic school because I thought that such a decision would prove to be very important.

After a few weeks of visiting several schools in the area, Steve called to say that Jason liked St. Joseph's Academy. I asked Jason to describe the school to me. He took great pains to provide details. First, he liked the homes surrounding the area. He noticed the neat, clean yards and well kept houses. He told me how the streets were nice and clean and that there wasn't any trash or litter about. St. Joseph's Academy was about 15 minutes away from the group home and it was set in the middle of the block. I listened to each detail in earnest. I really wanted Jason to be in a safe, nurturing environment where he could spread his wings and soar academically, socially, and emotionally.

I was so glad that a decision had been made and could sense a slight ray of hope and assurance in Jason's spirit.

The next day I picked up Jason from the group home and we visited the school together. Jason's grades were poor. He had failed a number of subjects. However, I knew he needed a chance to attend another type of school in another type of environment. On our short journey to St. Joseph's Academy, our conversation was light hearted. I didn't want to cause any anxiety. It was a new school and experience for both of us.

We pulled up in front of the school and it was just as Jason had described it—a solid structure that probably had been built around the turn of the century. The red and rust colored bricks loomed before us. The church steeple stood erect and sturdy in the afternoon sun. The surrounding grounds were neat. It seemed that meticulous care had been taken to maintain and preserve the history and heritage of St. Joseph's. I really felt that this was a place where Jason could flourish and blossom into a better student. I had taught in the public school system for many years, but a Catholic school symbolized discipline, order and faith. These elements were strongly evident inside and out.

There were no children in attendance that day. We entered a side door of the school and after a few comments from the secretary, I was directed to the main office and Jason to an adjoining room. A few moments later, I met the principal who ushered me into her small, uncluttered office. She offered me a seat. I noticed that books were neatly arranged on a shelf behind her desk and a crucifix was hanging on the wall. The curtains were blowing gently from an open window. The floors were sparkling and buffed to perfection.

Sister Maria was an elderly lady with snow white hair. Her eyes focused directly on me as she listened intently to my comments and concerns. She was not overly friendly, but she wasn't aloof or distant either. She appeared neutral; a position I readily accepted.

I explained my relationship with Jason and his lot in life. I also related facts about my interest in his education and making sure that he finished elementary school. There were several mentions of the group home where he was living, but I kept all comments objective and positive. I stated my intention to be supportive and to cooperate with his teachers to help him succeed, given the opportunity. Sister Maria sensed my sincerity and smiled slightly when I related some of Jason's interests and favorite things. I had to be compelling and state my case with strong conviction.

After about forty-five minutes, Sister Maria invited Jason to join us. I acknowledged him briefly and sat nervously in

Jason: Ward of the State

the hard chair near her desk. My fingers were crossed and I held my breath as Jason answered her questions. I really wanted him to make a good impression. I could tell that Sister Maria was carefully taking every detail into account. Jason answered each question to the best of his knowledge and with each answer, I could see her attitude soften. Sister Maria decided to admit Jason to St Joseph's Academy on probation. She stated that if his grades improved, he would be allowed to stay. I breathed a sigh of relief.

Earlier in the interview, I had mentioned to Sister Maria that Jason admired Michael Jordan and loved basketball. Not long after he had settled in, Jason tried out for the basketball team and made it. He was even elected captain. Jason was the only African-American on the team, but he felt a sense of pride and belonging. His uniform was blue and the number on his jersey was seven. He wore his uniform proudly and his face beamed when his team was mentioned. He was so happy. Basketball became an incentive to work harder—on and off the court. Being captain gave him lots of responsibilities, and he took winning seriously. He would yell orders and calls to his teammates as he dribbled the ball up and down the court and his teammates responded to his directions. His coach was very calm and treated his players with utmost respect.

Jason was a natural leader. I could see fierce determination on his face as he moved around the court. He had to win not only for his team, but for himself.

On one occasion, I asked Jason if he would like some of the boys from the group home to attend one of his games. He wasn't too sure that he wanted them there, but he did have a friend at the group home named Eddie, and it would be alright for him to go. I was glad that at least one person could share this experience with him.

Jason took the school bus to school but needed a ride back to the group home after a game. Therefore, I made an effort to attend as many games as possible and when I couldn't, Steve, the supervisor, would transport Jason. Many of the games were very heated and intense and Jason's team usually lost. During the car ride back to the group home Jason didn't say a word. He was stubborn. Even when they tried hard, they lost. Since he was the captain of the team, I tried to encourage him to see that winning wasn't everything. I told him to think about the next game and strategies for winning that one. My comments were made in earnest but I couldn't get a response out of him. He was too disappointed, and for him, losing meant much more.

Obstacles

Once while riding back to the group home, I told Jason a story that I had heard earlier that day at a conference I had attended. It was about a woman who had had a child late in life.

The conference had begun with the speaker showing the audience a pair of gym shoes. She asked us to observe the shoes then tell her something about them. Some people said the shoes looked worn, the laces were untied, they looked like boy's shoes, etc.

After hearing a variety of responses, the speaker slowly began her story of a boy who was blessed with lots of energy, so much so that his mother didn't know how to handle it. One day she was talking to a friend about it and the friend suggested that she enroll her son at the nearest park district. It seemed like a good idea so the woman took her son, Greg, to the park and registered him for track. She thought that running would wear him out and use up some of his energy. Sure enough, Greg became the best runner on the team. He was so tired after track meets that he would come home, eat dinner, and then rush off to bed.

At one of the track meets, Greg's mother stood behind the fence with the other parents, cheering their children on.

Jason: Ward of the State

After the starting whistle blew, the children began running with all their might and Greg was in the lead. His mother saw him out in front, turning the corner for the final lap. In what seemed like a second later, Greg stumbled and fell just inches shy of the finish line. His mother could not believe it. She ran out to the field where he lay on the ground, unhurt but deeply disappointed. She leaned down and asked, "What happened? Are you okay?" The boy responded that his shoe lace had come untied and he tripped on it.

On hearing this, his mother became angry and screamed, "You lost the race because your shoe lace became untied? You denied me a trophy and the pride of your winning the race because of a shoe lace?"

The crowd became silent. Greg felt crushed as well as defeated. With downcast eyes, his mother realized what she had said, but it was too late. She was ashamed. She reached down and embraced Greg, telling him that winning wasn't everything and she was glad that he wasn't hurt.

The speaker hesitated a few minutes, painfully aware that the audience knew she was the mother in question. Her story had deeply touched the audience. She went on to say that the shoe laces were an obstacle, but one that could be overcome. Obstacles cause people to stumble and fall. The key is to get up and start again with purpose and conviction. Her overall message was: stop, think and focus on achieving your goals in life, no matter what the obstacles.

I wanted Jason to learn from this story, but he wasn't in the mood for it. For the rest of the drive I respected his wishes and said as little as possible, all the while thinking that whatever it would take, Jason and I would reach the finish line together.

Jason: Ward of the State

College Admission

Jason was not having an easy time. Even with his commitment to basketball, his world was still unstable. Every day, he was reminded that he was a ward of the state, without family and foundation.

At St. Joseph's Academy, I stayed in close touch with his teachers. When I picked up his very first report card, the teacher spoke highly of his abilities but poorly about his academic progress. She said that he was having problems focusing. He did like art and physical education but had little interest in other subjects. This concerned me deeply. Another of his teachers said that Jason was very smart and intelligent but didn't apply himself. Just staying in school was a constant struggle for him.

I understood Jason's conflicting emotions. His personal life spilled over into his academic world. The longer he lived at the group home, the more he suffered.

We faced obstacle after obstacle together and I kept in constant touch with his teachers, but he was barely hanging in there. What a heavy burden he was carrying, but what were his alternatives? His hurts were my hurts. His disappointments were my disappointments. At one point, I was afraid that he would run away. He was hanging by a thread, but he promised me that he would graduate from St. Joseph's and I believed him. My heart ached at the sight of him.

Kevin began his senior year as Jason entered eighth grade. Kevin wanted to go to college, but he had missed getting the information he needed to apply. It had been a very long time since I had to deal with preparing for college, and I was just as lost as to how to get started. So I called and made an appointment with Kevin's counselor. Kevin met me there and the counselor was helpful. I also took Kevin to a private college counselor because I needed help in order to assist him. As we sat with this counselor, I could tell that

Jason: Ward of the State

Kevin wasn't aware of how much work is required to get into college. We left her office with a list of steps to follow.

During his senior year, Kevin continued to take classes that would improve his grades and give him an opportunity to develop college admission test taking skills. The school year was passing rapidly and there were deadlines to meet.

Kevin took several college entrance exams. Each time he waited patiently to hear how he had done. I enjoyed helping him read through the reference materials and fill out applications. I was sure that Kevin could get into a city college, but I wanted him to go away to school so that he would be in a safer environment and able to concentrate on learning and studying.

My sister, Connie, and I helped Kevin compose a cover letter to accompany his applications. I wanted the colleges to see him as an individual with multiple needs and concerns and not just a number. I was sure that writing a personal note about his experiences would give him a better chance. The waiting game was full of anxiety, anticipation and a test of patience.

Finally, he got the call. It was good news. He had been accepted by a private Illinois university. He was thrilled.

Graduation

June 1998 was a busy, exciting month. Kevin graduated from high school in a huge auditorium. I and one supervisor from the group home were in attendance. Kevin invited some of his friends to join us after the ceremonies to celebrate at a local restaurant. In the fall Kevin would exit the group home and head off to college.

In the meantime, Jason had completed elementary school. It was a milestone and I never thought this day would happen. Though they were only two years apart in age, Jason had fallen behind in school while Kevin had started school at a younger than average age. Graduation day for Jason was June 5—a beautiful summer afternoon. The sky was a vivid blue, Jason's favorite color.

As I drove to the old St. Joseph's Catholic Church, my thoughts were of the difficulties Jason had overcome to get this far. I became sad when I thought about his struggles, but Jason had made it.

It takes a lot of preparation to get a child ready for graduation. I had given Steve money to purchase all of the clothing Jason would need—shoes, shirt and tie and all of the incidentals. Steve took care of everything.

I also told Jason to purchase something special for himself. He deserved a special gift to mark this occasion. But Jason put the money aside until I could take him to a Flea Market. We did that one Saturday. He looked at clothing, games, cameras, etc. but to my surprise, Jason settled on a silver cross and chain. I saw the cross as something spiritual but I could tell that Jason wanted it because wearing a cross and chain was a fad at that time. Either way, it is one of the items he has treasured.

Jason's graduation class was small. They all looked so proud and dignified in their caps and gowns. The girls and boys were lined up outside the church according to height. Jason was one of the tallest students so he was toward the end of the line. I could feel his eyes searching for me before the processional. I caught his glance and smiled brightly. He returned my smile with a broad grin.

When it was time for them to enter the church, I adjusted my video camera to capture every moment. As he marched down the aisle with his classmates, I had a hard time holding back tears and steadying my camera. After the mass, there was a speaker who reiterated some of the same philosophy I had ingrained in Jason about staying in school and keeping focused on the future.

Finally, the diplomas were handed out. Jason walked up and extended his hand to take his diploma. He was beaming. Following a wonderful ceremony, we went to dinner with several of my nephews who had accompanied me to the graduation. Jason could order anything he wanted from the menu because this was his special day. That made him extremely happy. The entire evening was focused on him and his accomplishments.

Before Jason graduated, we had discussed high schools. To my surprise, he told me that he had taken the entrance exam for Cornell Preparatory High School, a private school on the west side of the city. I think he was influenced by other students at St. Joseph's. I was so glad that the Catholic school had made a difference in him. He really wanted to attend Cornell Prep. In order to do so, he would have to attend Cornell's summer enrichment program because his test scores weren't high enough. However, this didn't dampen his spirits or dull his mood. He passed every course and was allowed to enroll. It was a double milestone: Kevin entered college in September 1998 and Jason entered his freshman year at Cornell Prep. I settled down with my husband to enjoy the beautiful weather and activities of summer. But I was not at all prepared for the tragedy that was parked around the corner.

Suddenly, William Dies

My husband suffered a massive stroke and passed away on July 18. We had enjoyed a typical morning, nothing out of the ordinary. I fixed him a big breakfast. We took a short walk, and then later on he rested awhile. We had an aide who came to our home to sit with William, allowing me an opportunity to run errands and go to the grocery store. While I was gone, she gave William the lunch that I had prepared and left for him.

I was back by mid-afternoon. We watched TV for a while. William enjoyed the news, especially the national news. While I was preparing dinner he called some of his friends on the phone, which was relaxing for him. He was never out of touch with his friends because he made it his duty to stay in touch. His best friend, Jim, lived only a few blocks away. They spoke every day. Many of his calls were to friends who lived in cities all over the United States. Some went back to his childhood.

I prepared some of his favorites for dinner. We had roast beef, potatoes, fresh green beans, rolls, and a pitcher of cool ice tea. He always enjoyed my cooking and I enjoyed preparing our meals, which he appreciated. He complimented me on a regular basis. After dinner we went for a short walk. He said that he always felt better when he walked a little after eating. The doctor had said that it was good for his health. Usually during these walks we would talk a while, then rest a while.

At some point between dinner and bedtime, something went amiss. I called 911 for an ambulance. My heart was beating fast. I was holding William's hand and trying to stay calm for his benefit, yet it became more and more difficult with each passing moment. I had been through this before, and I knew he was in urgent need of medical care.

William was rushed to the nearest hospital. They ushered me out of the ER cubicle. I was pacing back and forth outside the curtain. The medics were trying to stabilize his condition. Hour after endless hour stretched by. It seemed like forever before my husband was transferred to a hospital room. I walked next to him while they moved him, telling him "everything is going to be okay." In my heart I was praying for that. The doctors told me to go home and get some rest. I was so disturbed by the sudden change in his condition that rest was the farthest thing from my mind, yet I knew I wouldn't be of any use to anyone if I didn't rest. So I decided to lay down for a few minutes on a cot that was provided by the hospital. It seemed like only seconds had passed when a rush of doctors and nurses entered William's room. They were working feverishly on my husband. The doctor came out of the room and spoke some words to me I will never forget. He needed an immediate response from me. I was flooded with emotions, panic stricken and numb. When I entered William's room again, I spoke to my husband in a whisper. He didn't recognize me. His bed was slightly elevated and he was looking up at the ceiling as if it were a black hole in outer space. His face was totally blank. I fled from the room, crying uncontrollably. The nurses rushed to my side trying to calm me down and settle my nerves. A part of my soul died with him that day.

Grieving hurts. I knew that I had to allow my emotions to run their course, but it was a very difficult time. My husband had anchored my life. Jason and Kevin had been a part of our lives, but William was my rock. They saw my husband as a role model and someone who cared about them and tried to help them. He was a kind and giving man, mild mannered and soft spoken. Yet in his own quiet way, he was a powerful person. He gave his time, talents, and resources unselfishly to help others; he believed in giving back to society. So when Jason and Kevin entered our lives, he embraced them and welcomed them into our hearts and home.

Oftentimes, he would share stories with the boys about growing up in Mississippi. He told them about his ride up north to Chicago to attend law school. He shared with them why he felt that education was so important and about his experiences as a lawyer and the importance of being honest. He was always encouraging them to do their very best in school. Reflecting on these conversations brought tears to my eyes, yet I had a sense of peace knowing that his words and deeds had touched so many people.

After his death, I read some of William's papers, including personal thoughts he had written after he retired from the bench. When he first became a judge he wrote, "I wonder if I have the necessary temperament to be a judge." He wrote about needing to be patient, fair, impartial and just in his decisions. I thought about all of the questions he posed to himself and realized that, though he rarely showed it, the weight of the world was sometimes on his shoulders. William had been an outstanding judge and an outstanding person as well.

Planning my husband's funeral was all consuming. I had difficulty focusing on the minute details and was glad to have my sisters and friends helping me. It took a lot of strength to carry on. It seemed like such a huge task to call William's family, friends and associates and plan the program at a time when my heart was heavy and I was grief stricken.

I wasn't sure of how Jason and Kevin would respond to news of William's death. They had so many issues of their own. I wondered if they would worry about whether I would continue to be there for them. This was a major loss in my life. I wanted to comfort them, but I was grieving deeply and wasn't sure about the future or anything else.

In the days leading up to the services, Jason and Kevin dragged around the house watching my every move. They looked dazed and lost. As the program was being prepared I asked the boys if they would like to say something. I was really trying to include them in everything. To my surprise, Kevin said yes, so their names were placed in the program.

At the appropriate time, both boys went up and stood in front of the pulpit, looking pale and scared. Kevin shared thoughts about how my husband had touched their lives. Jason was hidden a little by the pulpit. He didn't say anything. Listening and watching the boys made me realize that I needed them as much as they needed me. I knew right then and there through tears and sorrow that I would continue to help them. To me, it was such a courageous and charitable act to stand in front of the congregation and give such a glowing tribute. It warmed my heart and reaffirmed my commitment to them.

The funeral services were held on Thursday night and Friday morning. On Monday morning I drove Kevin to college for a two-day freshman orientation. Kevin felt the deep pain and sadness I was going through. He tried to keep our conversations light and engaging as we drove to his college. I was glad to spend time with him because it gave me a purpose. Kevin had exited the group home, therefore he had all his belongings with him. The car was loaded. I sat with all the parents and incoming freshmen, listening to speakers I can only vaguely remember. I was there to support Kevin as he began his new experience in college. It was important for him not to be alone, but I couldn't wait for the next day to come so I could leave. Kevin hugged me and waited until I got safely to my car before he turned in the direction of the school. I was holding on to the steering wheel tightly, watching him walk toward the college until he was a faint blur in the distance. My fingers were getting numb. I gripped the steering wheel to hold back the tears. Kevin looked back several times, waving "good-bye."

I thought about Jason as I drove home. The impact of his being left alone in the group home had eluded me. I was wrapped up in my own grief and being thrust into widowhood. I wasn't thinking about Jason and his continuing situation. I knew he hated the group home and all the things associated with it. The rules and regulations made him feel like a prisoner. Now Kevin was off to college and Jason was left to fend for himself.

Jason Leaves the Home

When I returned home, I learned that Jason was having a difficult time without Kevin. Kevin had been his only family member, there to support him and look out for him. It was no surprise that Jason's feelings of abandonment intensified after Kevin left.

A few days later, I received a call from one of the supervisors inquiring about Jason's whereabouts. I could give them no information. Where could he be? How could I find him?

I was worried sick thinking about the dangers he could encounter. There were all types of pitfalls out there. The city streets were no place for any child, especially Jason. Then one evening, I received a call from him. I was thrilled to know that he was alright, but I could hear a great deal of uneasiness in his voice. He called to let me know that he was doing fine. I thought about having him live with me, but I didn't think it would work at the time. I encouraged him to go back to the group home for his own safety. My comments fell on deaf ears. He had made up his mind and he was determined to go out on his own.

When Jason left the group home, I didn't know that he had gotten his step-grandmother to sign as guardian for him. He wasn't living with her. Even if he were, Jason would still be in the "System," still a ward of the state. But the "System" was unaware of his whereabouts. I knew this because of the numerous telephone calls I received from social workers and the group home supervisors who were still looking for him.

This disturbed me quite a bit. Jason was out there and I couldn't reach him. The social workers and I would see Jason at school but he disappeared when school was out. Jason was clothed in a shroud of secrecy. Since he had left the group home and was not with his grandmother, Jason had decided to keep his whereabouts secret from me and everyone else.

Over the next year, I didn't know where Jason was living, nor did I hear from him very often. He was still enrolled at Cornell Prep but he was having serious attendance problems. I was engulfed with worry, fear and anxiety for his safety. Each time the phone rang, I hurried to answer it, hoping it would be Jason. I had many sleepless nights, tossing and turning, wondering where he was and what he was doing.

Jason: Ward of the State

Because he was not attending school regularly, Jason was suffering academically. He was doing just enough to get by. The only time I could see him was at school. The Cornell teachers, especially Mr. Johnston, Jason's counselor, were constantly asking me to come to school for conferences about Jason. He would wait in the adjacent office while we discussed options and ways to handle the situation.

Whenever I saw Jason at school, I would observe him closely for signs of abuse or neglect. I was very concerned about his health and safety, but all I noticed was that he wasn't properly groomed. His uniform was dirty and he was sleepy and tired. Other than that, nothing appeared to be out of the ordinary. I kept reassuring him that I was there for him and I would never let him down.

I recalled one conversation during this stressful period when he told me that he had been on his own and he was making it. I could see in his eyes that he was troubled, but he seemed oddly in control of the situation. My imagination was running wild with worry and concern each time we spoke. He told me over and over that this is what he wanted to do. I believe that Jason remained in school and out of trouble because I had supported him for years and he knew I was there for him now. I didn't want to lose him at any cost.

I continued to pay his tuition even though he might be in school only one or two days a week. I was constantly on edge. On one occasion Jason said, "If you don't hear from me that means I'm okay." I had to believe him but that didn't stop me from worrying night and day. My friends knew I always answered the phone no matter how late at night because it might be a call from Jason.

At least when Jason was in school I knew he was in a safe environment. Many sessions with Mr. Johnston gave me insight into his situation. I knew he would receive the support he needed at Cornell but any intervention beyond that was out of our hands. Jason's teachers related how respectful he was when he was in class and that made me feel somewhat better. I became a regular fixture at the school, following up in his progress and checking on his attendance. It was the only way I could stay connected.

During one of my meetings with the staff I mentioned that these school visits ran against my philosophy about good parenting. The teachers knew I believed in the power of education and a cooperative effort with a child's teachers. When parents monitored their child's daily assignments and kept in touch with his or her teachers, they would only visit school for report card pick-up. But this wasn't the case with Jason. He wasn't the typical student and he didn't have a typical family situation. It gave me purpose to check on him and stay abreast of everything concerning him. Unfortunately, Jason's personal life was having a direct impact on his schooling. He was failing and reports from his teachers were not good.

His safety and general well being were so compromised that school had become less important to Jason. Staying in touch with his teachers helped me maintain some semblance of sanity.

A turning point came when I received an urgent call from a hospital. It was a week day evening when the telephone rang. The person on the other end stated his name and said, "I am calling from a medical center and do you know Jason...?" I told him that I did. All the while my heart was pounding. I was sure something terrible had happened. "Is Jason all right?" I was assured that he was. This person said that Jason had walked into the medical center seeking help because he was depressed. He told me that Jason had given him my phone number. I asked if I could do anything to help, then I asked to speak to him. The conversation was brief. Jason said that he was okay. I reassured him that if he needed me for anything I was going to be there for him.

At school I was trying to hold things together. I had conversations with the principal and his teachers. They sympathized and understood Jason's situation but how long could they tolerate his failing grades and absenteeism? He was not telling anyone his whereabouts, and they were concerned. At one point a counselor suggested finding another group home for Jason, one that was closer to school. I knew that I could never convince Jason. Furthermore, I knew that such a move wouldn't solve his mounting emotional problems. It was only a matter of time before he would be expelled. I began to give up hope. Jason probably thought that he was doing the best he could and would somehow make it, but I was beginning to feel that maybe it was time to let go. There was only so much that I could do.

A Happy Surprise

I went up to the school on the last day before the Christmas break to tell Jason about where my family was having Christmas dinner and to invite him to attend. He wasn't there that day and I had no way of reaching him. I left the school thinking, "Why bother to Christmas shop for him since I won't be seeing him during the holidays?" To my utter surprise things turned out differently from anything I ever could have imagined.

Kevin contacted me and asked to join my family for the holidays. I was thrilled to see him. My sister was hosting our Christmas dinner. On Christmas day, before driving over to my sister's home, Kevin asked me to stop at his grandmother's house for a minute. I knew Jason wasn't living there so I had no hope of seeing him. Kevin made small talk as we traveled to his grandmother's and pointed out a rather large Christmas tree at the end of the block. The tree was in the center of the front yard of someone's home. I pulled up to the curb to take a closer look at a gorgeously decorated tree, rising up from a neighborhood in decay. It stood in defiance of its environment. It was firmly anchored with sturdy ropes. Ornaments were scattered about the branches and shiny strings of silver and gold garland encircled its perimeter. There were strings upon strings of lights. It was the most beautifully decorated house on the sparsely decorated block. "You're right, Kevin," I said. "I should pay closer attention to the beautiful decorations and lights." But my mind was preoccupied. Where was Jason and what could he be doing? I forced myself to think about the good things as we got closer and closer to our destination.

As I was pulling up to their grandmother's house, I turned off the ignition and touched the button to unlock the door. Then out walked Jason with a large black garbage bag in his hand. I was thoroughly surprised. He came up to the car, reached in, handed me the garbage bag and said, "Merry Christmas, Mrs. Peterson!" I was shocked. I couldn't believe what I was seeing. "Jason, how have you been?" "I've been doing okay, Mrs. Peterson. I wanted to surprise you and wish you a Merry Christmas." His jacket was too light for the cold weather and he wasn't wearing a hat. I still couldn't believe my eyes. "Jason, thank you so much." He smiled even wider than before.

I felt terrible that I didn't have a present for him. I should have gotten him something. When I looked over at him again his mood had changed. Suddenly, he appeared melancholy. It seemed that he couldn't contain his grief. I believe that he knew he had let me down by not attending school regularly and not staying in touch.

I reached over and hugged him tightly and said, "I have done everything in my power to keep you in Cornell Prep and now it's up to you to get back in school." I told him that I would continue to pay tuition and support his efforts if he remained in school. The freezing, blistery, wintry air was slapping us in the face. Jason exhaled and looked relieved that I hadn't given up on him.

"I'll do better," he said meekly. I wanted to believe every word he was saying but the look on his face changed even more when he said, "I promise I will get back in school." I nodded that I understood but there were miles between us at this juncture.

I knew that Jason wasn't staying at his grandmother's house but Kevin had carved out a little surprise which had turned into a wonderful, poignant moment. I looked at my watch. It was getting late. Kevin and I had to make haste to get to my sister's house on time. Jason lingered at the curb looking sad and lonely. When we reached the end of the block, I glanced back and saw him walking toward the apartment building. I prayed that he would be okay and stay out of harm's way.

As we drove, I learned from Kevin that he knew very little about their grandmother. I asked why she wasn't helping Jason, but a small voice told me to be still, say little and expect less. Snow was beginning to fall as we arrived at my sister's house. The house was blazing with bright lights and candles in the windows. The house next door had a big plastic Santa sitting in the front yard. Animated white reindeer were moving their heads to and fro. Connie always had that big wide wreath taking up most of the doorway and window. I rang the bell. Connie came to the door, cheery and happy to see us. Hugs and kisses were in order and she told us to hurry in from the cold. Kevin went in first and I followed. Turning back to check the car, I saw a little boy and his parents walking past my sister's home, loaded with gifts. They seemed so happy. They waved at me then disappeared into another house. I thought about Jason and how he would be spending Christmas. My heart dropped for a minute. As I entered the hallway to remove my coat, I closed my eyes and secretly hoped Jason would have a nice day.

Later that evening after Kevin and I returned home from Christmas dinner, I turned on the radio to listen to some Christmas music and settled into a chair next to the Christmas tree. I was curious as to what had made the bag from Jason so heavy. I looked in and saw gifts wrapped in

Christmas paper. I took out the larger gift first and unwrapped it. I was stunned. It was a medium sized oriental lamp with a beautiful plastic shimmer around the top. Then I pulled out a rectangular gift, wrapped in the same decorative paper. I tore it off and there in my hand was a large framed picture of Jason leaning on a huge number 1998. He was wearing a white shirt and dark tie and his Afro looked neat. But it was the smile on his face that captured my heart. Tears begin to stream down my face. I thought of all that Jason had been through. He was still able to smile. In my mind, I was giving up on him and he was reaching out.

Whatever it took, Jason got himself back in school. He had to face the administration himself and plead his own worthiness to be readmitted. I knew that it was not going to be easy for him, but the school was the best environment for him. He was safe, his friends were there and the teachers were very supportive of him. Unfortunately, it was very difficult for him to catch up on all the course work that he had missed. As a result he failed his freshman year. Probably in most situations similar to Jason's, a student would have to transfer to another school. But by the grace of God and a sympathetic principal, Jason was given a chance to repeat his first year at Cornell Prep. He had to attend summer school, but the most important thing at the time was that Jason was back.

Jason's Neighborhood

It wasn't until the second year of Jason living on his own outside of the group home that he allowed me to drop him off at certain locations that were near where he was living. Eventually, our contacts and encounters became more frequent. He didn't want to reveal details about where he was staying and I tried not to pry information from him. I was happy to be in his life again under his terms. Sometimes

Jason: Ward of the State

I would pick him up from school and we would go to a grocery store on the west side. He would select all of the items himself. The cart would be loaded. On the way home he would ask me to drive near a certain alley and drop him off there. This filled me with dread. He was so secretive about his whereabouts. I didn't know where he was going or with whom. It really bothered me to see him walking down that alley.

However, Jason knew his environment and how to survive in it. I imagined that if you had groceries it meant that you also had some money, then I would think about someone robbing him and taking his bags. It didn't seem fair that he had to fight for basic needs. Being discrete and overly cautious about his every action seemed to be turning into a matter of life and death. That was serious. I could sense the gloom and despair everywhere. Businesses in the area were dirty and graffiti covered the walls and fences. People were cruising up and the street with the car windows open, music blasting so loud that it vibrated and shook anyone or anything nearby. Glances that were cast your way were cold and uninviting. Groups of boys hung out on corners with nothing to do. It appeared that drug trafficking was constant. People were standing in the same locations every day, waiting and looking for drop offs or pickups. Money was exchanged in broad daylight. You could feel the violent tempo of the neighborhood. My heart skipped a beat every time I drove through it. It was overwhelming to me. I was very nervous, but I wasn't going to let the unwelcome glances prevent me from driving Jason home, wherever that may be. One message I tried to hammer into Jason was that his choices now were really critical. "If you live a life full of gangs and drugs and violence, a young death will be the result." I continued to emphasize the negative effects of living in the midst of senseless killings. It didn't seem to bother him. He had been numbed. He didn't even turn and look at me while I was delivering my strong point of view. Jason's silence said that nothing could possibly be worse than what was going on in his life right now, but I didn't really know what that was.

After a while, Jason glanced at me with pleading, sympathetic eyes and heart. He said that he didn't want to be like the people around him. "I couldn't stand around on a corner all day just waiting. That's not me." I knew he meant it. I told him, "Remember what you see here because one day it will be a thing of the past. You will be victorious." I wasn't absolutely sure of my words but I had to give him faith and the seeds of hope.

Eventually, Jason allowed me to drop him off in front of the place where he lived. The street was lined with sturdy, old gray stone houses. Most of them were standing firm against the test of time. Rusted black iron fences connected one yard to another. Tall squeaky gates swung open to barren courtyards and a few patches of grass. Vacant lots were strewn with litter and debris. Children were everywhere, running in and out of the streets and yards, not looking to see where they were going. The area was marked by signs of violence. This was not a safe, decent place to live and grow.

Cars were parked tightly on both sides of the street. If you doubled parked like I had to do to let Jason out, another car would squeeze by boldly as if to threaten and intimidate. No one could scare me because I was already completely frightened by the harshness of the neighborhood. You didn't want to cause trouble here because it could cost you your life. I was petrified at what could happen if I made a mistake, made someone angry. Therefore, I moved in and out of there quickly, ever mindful of the potential for disaster. It gave me some comfort to keep my cell phone in hand at all times. I had to be on guard. I still quiver at the thought of how often I drove though that area.

I had been Jason's teacher but over the course of a few years, I became the student and Jason the teacher about

Jason: Ward of the State

the life he was leading. On one occasion when I was taking Jason back to the west side, he told me about the "shut down" the police had ordered for a block near his house. I had no idea what he was talking about. The manner in which he related this situation led me to believe that it was a common event. I wanted to know exactly what a "shut down" meant. Jason calmly proceeded to tell me that the police would scan the area for illicit behavior and drugs and would search thoroughly for weapons. He told me he could see everything from his window. I listened intently to what he was saying because this was beyond what I thought a neighborhood should be.

Actually, not far from where he lived was a beautiful city park with flowers and well kept trees and bushes. The playgrounds were neat and clean. The children weren't running and playing in vacant lots with broken glass and litter. Just a few blocks away you could sense a different tempo. It was refreshing to know that there could be beauty in the midst of a war zone.

We were on a path to learn about each other's world. I had to imagine how the sights and sounds of his terrible neighborhood affected him and Jason in turn had to imagine how my world appeared to me. I did not want to alienate him from his surroundings, so I tried hard to keep my thoughts and opinions to myself, to remain neutral and not judgmental about the place he called home. I had to be patient and listen to Jason as he detailed the best shops and restaurants. He took pride in telling me about particular points of interest, along with the ugly aspects of the neighborhood.

The way Jason had adapted and become fully knowledgeable about his neighborhood was impressive. Sometimes, a faint smile would light up his face as he gave me his extra special tour! Chicago is such a large city. Jason made the streets, stores and other parts of his area come alive. It was becoming sort of an adventure.

Lucky Summer Break

During his sophomore year at Cornell Prep, Jason sang in the school choir. This was the first high school activity in which he participated, and it was a highlight for me. I attended concerts and other events on a regular basis. It was my way of supporting him and the school. Jason appeared at peace when he sang. The choir seemed to provide a sense of belonging and purpose.

On one occasion, the choir presented a concert at a major hotel in downtown Chicago. Jason had to travel with the rest of the students on the school bus. He had waited until the last minute to tell me that he needed a new uniform and tie to wear to the performance. I spent my day in heavy downtown traffic, running around in the rain to purchase these items. When I arrived at the hotel the students were trying to find the room where they were to gather before the concert. When the principal saw Jason she shouted, "Hurry and get up there with the choir. We need your voice!" Jason smiled broadly. He knew his part was important. Jason was a member of an organization and that in turn made him feel wanted and needed, which boosted his self-esteem and pride.

The choir sang old favorites with new arrangements. The choir director put his heart and soul into the music and it brought out the best in the students. Jason sang with such expression I could tell that he was truly alive and free. I always bought my video camera. I wanted the memories to last for years to come.

Toward the end of Jason's sophomore year, a glimmer of hope for ending his gloomy past appeared. Cornell Prep had a special summer program that offered the opportunity to go hiking in the mountains of Denver, Colorado. The purpose of the experience was to encourage self-discovery and give disadvantaged students a chance to explore and travel. Jason was selected to go. At first, he said no. He was still facing so many difficult issues in his personal life. Even though the trip to Colorado was a great opportunity, he didn't appear ready to embark on such an adventure.

One of my fears was the increase in violence that occurred during the hot summer months. I knew there would be more danger, especially for young males. This trip would be a diversion from living day after day in a turbulent area. I really wanted him get away and strongly encouraged the trip. The fact that he was selected to go made the trip even more appealing and important.

A meeting for parents and students who were taking the trip was held one Saturday morning. Because he didn't have a telephone, I made a special trip to school on the Friday before to remind Jason of the meeting. He said that he would be there even though he was still reluctant about going. That evening a friend and her son who were visiting from Florida went shopping with me for all the items on the list the school had provided. My trunk was full of blankets, warm clothes, flashlights, lanterns, backpacks and the like. I arrived at the meeting on time, eager to get the last minute details. As I was parking I saw Jason walking toward the school. He usually sported a large, fluffy Afro, so I was very surprised to see that his hair was braided in cornrows.

My friend and her son accompanied me to the meeting. As we entered the school building, the principal was coming down the hall. She took one look at Jason's hair and shouted, "Get out of here. You know the rules." I stood there shocked. He knew that his hair style would cause him to miss the meeting. I begged Jason to go home and come back with his hair combed. I even offered to drive him there to save time and leave my friend at school to take notes about the program. He agreed and we drove in silence. I was praying that he would recognize the importance of this trip and how it could change his life. I decided to pull over, stop the car and open the trunk to show Jason all the things I purchased for him to go on the trip. I thought that seeing all the gear would encourage him to go. I offered to wait in the car while he combed out his hair so that we could return to school for the remainder of the meeting. I was appalled that even after my encouragement and expense to get him ready for this trip he didn't want me to drive him back. "No, I'll walk back to school." At that moment I knew the trip was over and that he would miss a chance of a lifetime. All of my efforts had been in vain.

People were still in the auditorium when I returned. The coordinator wanted to make sure that everyone had the itinerary and directions. She thoroughly repeated what was expected of each parent and student. I couldn't concentrate on what she was saying because I was worried about Jason. We waited patiently for him to come back. It seemed like hours passed. Hopes of his returning faded. I stared down at my lap and clutched my hands tightly, praying that he would appear in the doorway. I knew that cornrows take a lot of time to braid in neat rows and patterns and they take even more time to take apart. How could he be back before the meeting was over?

I sent my friend's son to the door to watch for him. So much was wrapped up in this trip. This was an opportunity to see another world beyond the west side with its gangs and drugs. Jason had never let me down before. Now I was afraid that he would disappoint me.

As the meeting was about to end, in came Jason, walking down the aisle with my friend's son, looking wild with his hair sticking out from underneath a baseball cap. It looked like lightning had struck his hair. It was a sight, but I was relieved and overjoyed that he made it in time. Jason didn't let me down after all! A rush of emotions flooded over me as I struggled to compose myself. Everyone was shocked at his appearance but I was thrilled at seeing him.

It was the responsibility of the parents to get the children to the airport for the trip. The coordinator asked me to take another student along with Jason. I agreed enthusiastically and Jason was happy to have a buddy.

After the meeting, we drove around to buy the last essential items like film and batteries. I could tell that he had changed his mind and was excited about the trip, making sure that he had everything he needed for hiking.

I told Jason that I would pick him up at 5:00 a.m. on the morning of the trip. That was very early, but we had missed so many details that I didn't want to risk being late. I knew this was asking a lot but he agreed to the early departure and assured me that he would be ready. I couldn't call him, so I just prayed that he would wake up and that we would get to the airport on time.

I had barely pulled up to the corner when Jason appeared out of the darkness, eager and ready to go. He had been waiting for me in spite of the early hour. I was happy that he was on time. He jumped into the car and we then proceeded to pick up his classmate. Would Jason find out something new about himself hiking in the mountains of Colorado? Would this be a period of enlightenment? Would this trip renew his spirit in spite of the dire circumstances he was in? I pondered these thoughts as I watched the plane carry Jason into the sunrise.

Junior Year

Jason returned from his trip to Colorado invigorated, with a renewed sense of self-confidence and pride. He was now a junior in high school. The new school term began very well. Jason seemed more mature, resolute and resolved to prove himself—the same person, but with a different attitude. There was a spring in his step and he appeared lively and alert. The frequently somber expression had transformed into a vibrant, happy one. I was thrilled at the change. I'm sure that getting an A in both of his summer science courses also gave him confidence and a needed boost. The hiking trip had been a welcome respite from his anxiety and apprehension and to see him receive good grades on top of it was a triumph, indeed. Jason actually cut his hair to begin the new school year. He was pleased with himself and would sometimes break into a hearty laugh, which did him a world of good.

We got the supply list from the school clerk, a pleasant, middle-aged lady with a round face and short stature. She knew me by name. Other parents and relatives were in the office also, and I felt a sense of pride knowing that I was there to get Jason's supply list. The clerk was swamped, yet she paused when we came in and smiled. I acknowledged her look in my direction. The office was jammed with people trying to work their way into and out of the room. Both of us recognized previous classmates and spoke to several of them. Jason seemed very motivated about starting his junior year.

There were numerous textbooks to purchase along with study guides, paper, folders and the like in addition to the supply list we had picked up from the office.

About two weeks before school started, I had spoken to Jason about going school shopping. After his first day of class, I picked him up, driving through the parkway and around the school campus to the main building. Jason didn't disappoint me. He was standing outside, right on time.

It was a sunny day. I rolled down the window. "Hi, Jason. I'm so glad to see you. Have you been waiting long?"

Jason approached my car with his book bag securely on his back and a few books and folders in his hand. "Hello, Mrs. Peterson," he said, smiling. "They give us too much homework!" Jason exclaimed as we pulled off onto the main parkway and out of the school complex.

"What subjects are you working on?" I asked. I tried not to appear overly concerned about his school work, yet I was

Jason: Ward of the State

deeply involved in making sure that he did his assignments and kept up in school.

"I have Computer Technology, Algebra II, English Literature, and Earth Science. I have to take gym, art appreciation and a writing class. I hope I don't have to repeat any subjects." Jason said all this with strong feelings. I glanced at him from the corner of my eye. The teacher in me spoke, "Let me know if there is anything I can help you with." Jason looked over at me and grinned. I wanted to hear all about his assignments and course work, but I also wanted to keep my eyes and ears open for any signs of trouble or trauma.

We went on to talk about a special program that Cornell Prep was having for Career Day. Jason was happy to relay information about school events, but I could tell that he didn't want to deal directly with specific subjects or teachers.

Suddenly his mood changed. I could see a dark shadow forming. Jason was silent for a while but he bounced back when we stopped at a restaurant. Eating out was a special treat that we both enjoyed. Most of the time, he would order a hamburger and fries.

It was painful to watch Jason's mood changes. We could be having a great time eating at a restaurant or shopping and then it would happen. Sometimes I instinctively knew when to speak and when to listen and sometimes I didn't. I had to watch and wait for signs and signals. On many occasions, I wanted to permeate the dark clouds, to reach down and block the true source of his despair. I tried to keep up with his classes, teachers and school, but it wasn't enough. It never was enough to fill the void.

We had come so far, yet the future was still fuzzy. I tried not to dwell on any time but the present. Jason was now half way through high school. Anyway, we purchased most of the basic items and a few other things that he liked, most of which were of different shades of blue. Blue wasn't particularly my favorite color but over time, I found myself liking the color more and more. That first semester went well. I didn't have to attend as many parent/teacher meetings and his teachers were happy with his renewed interest and attitude. I felt relieved.

Steve

I couldn't believe that Jason had made it successfully through the first semester of school without any serious incidents. He was progressing well in all of his subjects. In October and November there were no significant challenges. Then December and January approached with the usual holiday fanfare and festivities. After the Christmas holiday and the New Year, Jason kept pace with his class work. February and March went well also, with only a few minor adjustments to the increasing pressures of high school. His attendance had improved and I didn't receive many calls concerning tardiness, incomplete assignments, or homework. I received his progress reports and I was pleasantly pleased and relieved. Yet with each passing day, I expected the bubble to burst. When it happened, I knew I would be faced with issues above and beyond my control.

In early April I got the call. "Hello, Mrs. Peterson. This is Mrs. Kelly calling from Cornell Prep. We are having a problem with Jason." I froze in my tracks and held onto the receiver tightly. After a few moments I asked, "What type of problem are you having?" She went on to say, "It appears that Jason has been absent from school quite a lot lately and we can't seem to contact him or get a note as to why he is absent. We wanted to notify you first so that we can solve this problem." I was mortified.

How could this happen when things were finally turning around? I could hear the school loud speaker in the background. "How many days has Jason missed?" I asked. "You will probably need to come to school to talk to the school counselor so that we can discuss this problem." I said, "Fine, I will be up there tomorrow morning." I hung up the phone and stared blankly at the wall. I flopped down in a chair and exhaled deeply, unaware of what could have changed the course of events.

The rest of my evening was spent in fear. What could be causing this drastic change in Jason's behavior? This question kept turning over and over in my mind. The television program I was watching became just noise so I turned it off and got ready for bed. Sleep was difficult. I lay in my bed imagining all sorts of situations. After a while, I drifted off but not without a silent prayer that things would be alright.

The next morning, I went to Cornell Prep to meet with Mrs. Davison, the school counselor. She ushered me into her sparely decorated office. I briefly closed my eyes in prayer. "Please, God, help Jason and give me the strength to carry on."

I was directed to sit in a chair in front of Mrs. Davison's massive desk. "Mrs. Peterson, Jason is missing school again and we need to address this problem. He is now a junior and more is expected of him. He cannot continue this and be able to finish high school with his peers." I looked at her drawn face and the numerous wrinkles etched in her brow. "I understand that Jason is missing school," I said weakly. "I can't give you a reason because I really don't know what is wrong. He had been doing so well the first semester and I thought that he would continue to do well the second semester. I don't know what else to say."

The walls were beginning to close in and the wide office now appeared to be a narrow passageway. I really didn't know where he was. All I wanted was to keep him in school at any cost and keep the lines of communication open.

Mrs. Davison was aware of my mounting frustration. She began flipping through Jason's attendance records and scores and shook her head. "Mrs. Peterson, you understand

Jason: Ward of the State

our position at Cornell Prep. We demand a certain level of competence and achievement that we will not compromise."

I sat there, unable to explain further about his absenteeism when the phone rang. Mrs. Davison answered the phone and to our surprise, it was Jason.

"Hello," Mrs. Davison said. "Jason, I can't believe it's you! Mrs. Peterson is here. We were just having a discussion about your missing school so much this term. What seems to be the problem?" There was a long silence on the other end of the phone. Mrs. Davison looked over at me. Her eyes were wide with wonder like mine were. I sat on the edge of my seat tying to hear bits and pieces of the conversation. Then she asked Jason if he wanted to talk to me. Jason said, "Yes." I distinctly heard his resounding answer and it made me glad that I was there at the right time and place to receive his call.

"Jason," I said, "what seems to be the problem?" I could feel the tension in his voice. "Mrs. Peterson, Steve has been ill. He has cancer and he's been really sick. Eddie and I have been over here taking care of him." "Over where?" I knew when I said it that it didn't really matter. He was safe and had a viable reason for this turn of events. Mrs. Davison looked puzzled. "Who is Steve?" She didn't remember his name on Jason's school records and he wasn't the adult who came to school to see about his progress.

I had to respond to her puzzled look quickly and explain who Steve was. At the same time, I wasn't prepared to ask Jason too many more questions because I knew he would go into his secretive mode. He was hesitant to answer anyway because he knew that Mrs. Davison was still in the room. "Jason, let me know how you are and if I can help in any way." Jason said, "Okay" but before he hung up he mentioned that Steve was going into the hospital the next day and asked me if I would come to visit him. He told me that he would be admitted to Rush-Presbyterian Hospital on the west side tomorrow morning and that he had to see

Jason: Ward of the State

about him. I clearly understood his serious dilemma and the crisis situation that had been thrust upon him.

Jason had kept this secret from me and the school. Now his secretive world was falling apart. How could I not go to see Steve at the hospital? It appeared that Jason had been taking care of him for a considerable length of time. I could only imagine what hardships he had to endure trying to care for him while avoiding my probing questions and concerns. I had imagined the worst case scenarios about why he wasn't in school, and here he was taking care of a gravely ill person who had befriended him at the group home. It made me shudder to think of all the things he had to do while trying to go to school every day. He was still a child and the weight of the world was on his shoulders. Jason had been taking care of Steve all this time and I didn't know it. No wonder he had been missing school and fallen behind in his studies. No wonder he appeared exhausted and overwhelmed.

Mrs. Davison was staring at me with a worried expression. She was sitting very erect and rigid in her seat. Her folded hands and stoic demeanor suggested that she had the school's position to consider and not the entire situation. I didn't want to divulge too much information because I didn't want Jason to get into trouble. "Mrs. Davison, Steve was Jason's supervisor at the group home where he lived before coming to Cornell Prep." Mrs. Davison couldn't connect with what I was saying. "It is apparent that the boys have been living with Steve and caring for him while they were going to school." Mrs. Davison listened, but she still didn't see why two young boys had the responsibility of caring for an adult to whom they weren't related. I told her that the boys probably felt obligated to care for Steve since he was providing them shelter.

I then understood why Jason had been so secretive about where he was living. When Jason left the group home he probably went to stay with Steve. He had become a runaway. I sat in the chair a few more minutes, allowing the current change of events to sink in. I was totally shocked that Jason had to endure all of these hardships.

Mrs. Davison and I exchanged a few more comments about what strategy we would use to help Jason get back to school. But after that heart wrenching call from Jason, the school and academia took on a different focus. My heart was bleeding for Jason. He had been dealing with so many difficult issues in his short life. I didn't know what to do next, other than to see Steve and witness for myself how Jason was doing.

I left the counselor's office with a heavy heart, walked swiftly down the hall and out the side door to the parking lot. I couldn't find my car at first. When I finally found it I opened the car door, got in, grasped the steering wheel tightly, closed my eyes and prayed. I let out a few sobs and started the ignition. I don't remember driving but somehow I made it home safely.

It took a while to compose myself and calm down from the day's disturbing events. As soon as I set my purse on the table, the phone rang. "Hello, is this Mrs. Peterson?" The voice asked expectantly. "Yes, this is Mrs. Peterson. Whom may I ask is calling?" "This is Mrs. Rainer, Steve's mother. My son used to be a supervisor at the group home where Jason was residing." I nodded, even though she couldn't see me. "Mrs. Peterson, Steve is not doing well and I wanted you to know that he will be admitted to the hospital tomorrow morning. Would it be possible for you to come see him? He has asked about you." It took a few moments to register that this must indeed be a serious situation.

"How are you, Mrs. Rainer?" I asked slowly. "I spoke to Jason this morning. He told me about Steve's illness and how he had been taking care of him. I am so sorry to hear this news."

"My husband and I would appreciate it if you could come to see Steve. We see Jason frequently and he talks about you all the time. You are really special to him," she uttered

Jason: Ward of the State

softly. There was a muffled sound in the background and I knew that she was trying to keep from crying. I could hear the deep pain in her voice. A rush of sadness enveloped me. "Mrs. Rainer, I would be glad to see Steve and support you in any way that I can." I could hear a little lift in her voice when I said I would be there tomorrow. We exchanged good-byes and I hung up the phone.

I fixed a light dinner and retired to the living room to answer a few letters and catch up on my reading. The effort was fruitless. I couldn't concentrate so I went to bed early, not knowing what to expect, what to think or what to do.

I couldn't get Steve off my mind. I had met him many times at the group home. There were numerous other supervisors but Steve was my regular contact person. He was always professional and patiently took me through the steps and procedures required by the welfare system to assure that the boys were taken care of. They really liked him and it was evident that the feelings were mutual.

The Steve I remembered was a happy, upbeat man with deep brown skin that was flawless. He had dark brown hair that was closely trimmed and he always dressed neatly. He had a hearty laugh and a smile that would light a room. Steve's build and height were average, but his big, sparkling smile and warm, genuine personality made him extremely appealing. He always had a pleasant word and firm handshake that made the statement, "I value you as a person." Steve was a jewel and I could see why Jason was so fond of him. I tried to keep a healthy, positive picture of Steve in my mind but it was difficult considering the sudden turn of events.

The next morning I had trouble getting ready to go to the hospital. I couldn't make up my mind about what to wear. I certainly didn't want to wear something dreary. Finally I settled on a blue pantsuit with a brightly colored blouse. I gathered a few more belongings and went out the door.

Jason: Ward of the State

It was quite a long distance to the hospital. I walked into the reception area and a small, pleasant looking woman greeted me. She asked me the patient's name and told me that I needed a visitor's pass for room 328 on the third floor. I took the pass and walked down the hall to the elevator. I hesitated at the elevator, looking up at the tiled walls and stark white ceiling. I had a flashback to the hospital scene with William. I glanced down at the shiny, buffed, hard granite floor, my head low in silent prayer and contemplation. I was nervous.

I paused a moment before pressing the button to the third floor. I tried to visualize Steve standing before me happy and healthy. I really didn't know what to expect or even if I would recognize him. It had been many years since I had seen him and it was unsettling to imagine what his illness might have done to him.

The third floor was a swirl of activity. Nurses, doctors and staff were tending to patients, cleaning, distributing medications, walking in and out of patients' rooms, reviewing charts. A red light above one of the doorways was flashing and I could hear names being announced over a loud speaker.

I found Steve's room easily and stopped at the doorway to check the room number. Before me was a barely recognizable man. He was emancipated and pale. Thin, feeble hands were loosely clutching the top of the bedspread. His eyes were looking at me. I quickly checked the visitor's pass again to see if it matched the room number. Sadly, it did.

I was stunned. Steve gave me a slightly familiar smile. Those beautiful white teeth had been reduced to a glimmer, but I could see that this was the Steve I used to know. He recognized me right away. "Hello, Mrs. Peterson." he said weakly. "I'm so glad that you've come to see me." The powerful person I knew had gone. His whole face and body were smaller and he looked so sick. He was only a fraction of

Jason: Ward of the State

the man who had been Jason's supervisor. I hoped that he wasn't disturbed by my shock at seeing him in this condition.

"Hello, Steve," I said. I managed to smile brightly and hold his emaciated hand. I barely noticed at first that his parents were standing at the foot of the bed. I had interrupted their conversation when I entered the room. Mrs. Rainer said, "I am so glad that you could make it, Mrs. Peterson. Jason talks about you all the time. He and his friend, Eddie, have done so much for Steve and we're both so grateful that we have them in our lives." She looked fondly at her husband. I glanced back at Steve as he struggled to smile and look cheery. The same sparkle I knew before he became sick was still there, only the light was dimmer.

I managed to keep the conversation focused on what Jason was doing in school and some of his accomplishments. I shared a photo album that I had brought full of pictures of Kevin and Jason showing how they had grown over the years. Steve's face lit up as he feebly turned the pages of the album. One picture of Jason when he was about twelve years old got his attention. Jason looked so little. "Look at his haircut." I couldn't believe the metamorphosis myself. Browsing a bit further, Steve turned his head a little and I noticed him glancing at me. We shared a silent moment of understanding. I now knew how deeply Jason felt about Steve and he realized how fond I was of Jason. Steve rested his head on his pillow and exhaled deeply. He was lying very still with a contented look on his face. I spoke softly so as not to disturb him as I showed the album to his parents. He would wave his hand as if to gesture something about what I was saying but he was too weak to carry on a conversation. He was barely holding on.

I remember saying a few more words about Jason's hiking trip. "Did you know that Jason was chosen out of a large number of students to go on the hiking trip? He and one other student were selected to take part in this adventure," I said with as much emphasis as I could. Each time I mentioned a positive factor about Jason's school or accomplishments, Steve closed his eyes and smiled weakly. I could see that he was getting tired, so I prepared to leave. It was very painful to say good-bye to him in this condition. My heart was heavy as I thought about Jason's total commitment to Steve and his family and of the weight that Jason had carried on his shoulders for so long.

The third floor was filled with patients with very serious conditions. There was little noise or conversation coming from most of the rooms. Patients were lying in their beds barely moving, just existing. Several patients were hooked up to machines and many had tubes running in and out of their bodies. I passed the nurses' station and kept my head down as I looked for the way out of the hospital. The hallways seemed more confusing than when I had exited the elevator earlier. I followed the arrows and finally found the elevators. I returned my visitor's pass to the receptionist at the front desk and walked out to the parking lot and to my car.

On my way home, I thought about how extremely nice Steve's parents were. They truly loved their son and were very supportive. I was surprised that they knew so much about Jason. They spoke so favorably about his character. There were so many times that I had been in the dark, wondering about Jason and where he was living. I was glad that Mrs. Rainer had given me her telephone number. We now shared a special bond and connection.

In any event, I knew I had to prepare Jason for the worst. It was difficult talking about death and dying. I knew firsthand the pain of losing a loved one. I knew at the same time the importance of encouraging Jason to think about his future.

Another Lucky Break

The school term was nearing an end and summer was rapidly approaching. Special programs were being offered at Cornell Prep and one of them was the Summer Enrichment work program. I was thrilled that Jason was their number one candidate. Several members of the Foundation that worked with the school had interviewed fifteen students, but only two would be selected to spend nine weeks in Colorado. Jason had been so preoccupied with Steve and taking care of him that he had failed to mention to me that he was being considered for this wonderful opportunity.

I received a call from the school on Monday. "Hello, Mrs. Peterson?" I recognized her voice. "Jason has been selected to participate in the Summer Enrichment program. We need both of you to attend our orientation meeting to get the particulars about the trip and what is expected."

I was elated. The secretary went on to say that the meeting would take place on Wednesday morning at 9:00 a.m. in room 203. "I will be happy to attend the meeting, Mrs. Davison. Is there anything I need to bring?" She repeated the date and time and stressed the urgency of meeting the two men from the Foundation who would determine Jason's eligibility. I assured her that I would be there. My heart was leaping with gladness. Jason will be going to Colorado.

On Wednesday morning, I woke up early and got dressed. I looked outside my window to admire the bright, sunny sky. My spirits were soaring and I hoped Jason's were, too. He needed a diversion from Steve's illness and the stress of taking care of him.

The traffic was light as I drove to Cornell Prep. I made excellent time and arrived early. The receptionist directed me to have a seat in the lobby. I read a few magazines while waiting patiently for the meeting to start.

Jason: Ward of the State

At about 9:45 a.m. I was ushered into the conference room. Two gentlemen from the Foundation and the program coordinator, Mrs. Milano, were sitting at the solid oak table in the middle of the room. Mrs. Milano greeted me cordially. "I would like to introduce Mr. Randle and Mr. Gregory from the Foundation. They have been working with our school to provide learning and enrichment experiences for our students for this program. We were very impressed with Jason." I shook hands and smiled. "Jason really enjoyed the hiking trip last summer and I am thrilled that he is being considered again this year." Mr. Gregory motioned me to have a seat at the table to his right. "It is a pleasure to meet you, Mrs. Peterson. We have certain items to cover as part of our selection process. We want to interview Jason a second time so that he understands the commitment and responsibility involved in participating in this program." I nodded my approval.

I was very enthusiastic because if they selected Jason, it would be his first working experience. The boys would be trained to assist the grounds keepers and maintenance crew in the forest preserve. This was a real opportunity for them to demonstrate responsibility and a work ethic. I knew that some of the boys at his school would be grateful to be selected for this program because it would offer a chance for them to get away from troubled home environments and to learn valuable lessons. Getting paid for their work was an added bonus. I knew Jason would gain expertise and knowledge that would benefit him in the future.

The men began to sort through the papers before them. Mr. Gregory was a tall man with a slender build. He had soft blue eyes and sandy brown hair that was receding at the temples. He was wearing a blue shirt and stripped tie and was very distinguished looking. When he spoke of the students in the past who had participated in the program, Mr. Gregory smiled frequently and shared some experiences he had had as a boy in a similar program.

Mr. Randle, on the other hand, was short and average looking. He was very businesslike and spoke with authority. He wore a gray suit with a dark tan shirt, appeared somewhat impatient and checked the clock frequently. After a while, Mr. Randle asked, "Where is Jason? He is supposed to be at this meeting." It was about 10:30 by now. I squirmed nervously in my seat. I was unable to explain Jason's absence. Mr. Randle started to speak about the permission papers that had to be signed and how his time was valuable. Mr. Gregory asked, "Does Jason have any medical problems that you know of?" I responded that I didn't know. I proceeded to tell them about my relationship to Jason and that there were many things I didn't know about him and his family. Yet I wanted to speak on his behalf and describe his positive traits and character.

Mr. Randle was getting increasingly agitated about Jason's absence. He called the front office to see if he had arrived. Now I was getting worried. How could he disappoint me and the school? I watched as Mr. Randle spoke privately to Mr. Gregory about another meeting downtown and how his time was limited. After waiting ten more minutes, Mr. Randle uttered something in the nature of "other students who could benefit from this program if Jason isn't interested." I was getting more and more upset about him not showing up and the fact that he could lose out on this marvelous opportunity. Then Mr. Randle collected his belongings, excused himself and walked out the door.

I sat frozen in my seat. They needed a strong commitment from Jason and his absence made it appear that he wasn't interested.

Mr. Gregory and I sat staring at each other with questioning looks. I tried to let him know how important this trip was for Jason and how much he had enjoyed the program last summer. But by this time Mr. Gregory had begun looking at his watch, too. I didn't know what else to do. The minutes were ticking by and I couldn't stop them.

I closed my eyes and prayed silently "Please, God, let Jason come walking down the hallway." I had no way of contacting him. Suddenly, a clerk announced over the loud speaker that Jason was on his way. The coordinator had contacted Jason's friend, Ashley, and she in turn had called to remind him about the meeting. After she reached him, Jason called the office. I was so relieved that he hadn't forsaken me or the school.

I glanced at the clock. We had waited for almost two hours and tension was in the air but Jason didn't disappoint me after all! Instead of waiting impatiently in my chair, I went to the window to look for him. Some students were walking to class, others were sitting on a bench studying. Finally, Jason arrived looking sad and tired.

I knew the pressing issues and concerns he had were about Steve and his welfare and not the golden opportunity to participate in a working trip to Colorado. Jason entered the room and Mr. Gregory rose to greet him. "Jason, we were wondering if you were going to make it to school today." Jason looked pale and worried. He needed sleep and it showed in the deep, dark circles around his eyes and in his slumped shoulders.

"I had an emergency," he said softly. We exchanged glances as he moved slowly toward the table to sit down next to me and Mrs. Milano. Mr. Gregory motioned for him to sit next to him. He bent over, speaking to Jason privately in hushed tones. They talked back and forth about the importance of the trip and the need to be committed to fulfill all of the obligations. I heard Mr. Gregory explain to Jason that there wasn't any pressure for him to sign the forms because he could possibly be a candidate for the following summer. He carefully thought about his options and listened intently as Mr. Gregory spoke further about the requirements. His expression perked up a little but he was still seriously contemplating the matter.

Jason: Ward of the State

Jason had an important decision to make. All eyes were on him. Mr. Gregory waited. He appeared to be deeply concerned for Jason and gave him considerable time to think. Jason's eyes were pleading for understanding and sympathy. I smiled warmly, trying to ease the tension. To my amazement, he picked up the pen Mr. Gregory had handed him and signed the papers. My heart skipped a beat. He listened to Mr. Gregory reiterate some items about the trip. Then he shook his hand.

A faint smile was surfacing on Jason's face as his body relaxed a little. He exhaled deeply and looked at me somewhat relieved that this ordeal was over. I gave him a reassuring look to show my support for his decision.

Mrs. Milano had other permission forms and a list of supplies needed for the trip. She went over each form thoroughly and highlighted the areas to be signed. I reviewed the forms with Jason and we left the meeting on a positive note. He appeared eager to get back to Steve and I had another appointment that afternoon. I left the school feeling upbeat and happy.

About a week had passed after our meeting at the school when I received a telephone call from Mr. Gregory. "Mrs. Peterson," he said. "I just wanted to touch base with you to see if there are any questions you or Jason may have concerning the trip."

"It is so good of you to call. Jason is looking forward to the trip. I am so glad that you have faith in him." Mr. Gregory paused. "Did you get the supply list from Mrs. Milano?" I responded that I did. "Can I ask you a question, Mr. Gregory?" "Of course." "What made you stay and wait for Jason after Mr. Randle left?" I could tell that the question had caught him by surprise. There was a brief silence on the other end of the telephone. "I remember when I was young," Mr. Gregory said. "I saw potential in that young man from the first interview. He impressed us most over all the other students. I also saw how much faith

Jason: Ward of the State

you had in him. He is really lucky to have you in his life." "Jason is very special to me," I said proudly. Mr. Gregory made a few more comments about the students at Cornell and how schools have changed in the last decade.

I hung up and called the school to ask the clerk to notify Jason that I would pick him up after class tomorrow so that we could go shopping. Things were progressing nicely in the right direction, which eased some of my worries.

The next day, I arrived at the school minutes after class let out for the day. I spotted Jason outside the main school building carrying books in his hand as well as a full book bag on his back. It was a welcome change from the somber expression he had during the meeting last week. It was so good to see him happy and ready to go on our shopping excursion.

Shopping the second time around was a breeze. We knew exactly what type of clothing and gear to buy. He needed a larger duffel bag for his belongings so he could take more clothing on this trip. Jason seemed excited about going now. His face was aglow. He was also elated that we were going to stores on the west side of town. Sears was one of our first stops.

As we drove back through the area where he lived, Jason was deep in thought. We passed familiar houses, streets and parkways. This neighborhood of broken lights and vacant lots that shouted with neglect was home for him, a home I had to accept as well. I knew that getting away from the harshness of the area and the responsibilities that he had with Steve would give him a needed reprieve.

Jason was looking out of the car window. I said, "Jason, this trip will allow you to work and earn some money but you will also have lasting memories to treasure for a lifetime." Jason turned and looked at me slowly. He didn't say anything right away. He was looking straight ahead as we pulled up to the curb in front of Steve's house. "Mrs. Peterson, I am worried about Steve. He has been so good to

Jason: Ward of the State

me and Eddie and I hope he gets better." I responded, "We can't control things like sickness and death. We have to enjoy life for the moment and move forward. I am sure Steve wants you to learn as much as you can. I'm sure he will be okay." A slow smile started to appear on his face. He held his head down for a few moments as if in prayer and then said, "I will try and do my best." I knew he meant it and I reached for his hand and gave it a little squeeze for reassurance.

The students were to leave on Monday morning. I told Jason to set the alarm for 4:30 a.m. It would be dark that early in the morning. I drove up to the house and had barely parked when Jason bolted out the door and rushed toward the car.

I surveyed the area, ever mindful of the location. The streets were dark and empty. It was a very dangerous place to live and I always had to be careful. Jason knew I felt uneasy, especially at night. We loaded the duffel bag into the trunk of the car and headed to O'Hare Airport.

We drove part of the distance in silence. I handed him some extra spending money to take on the trip. He tucked the money safely in his wallet and said, "Thank you." This summer trip took place after the September 11th explosions at the World Trade Center in New York City so airport security was tight and extra time had to be allotted. I requested permission to accompany Jason to the gate. The reservations agent directed us to a specific window where permission was granted. We both felt lucky considering the circumstances and extra security and precautions. We walked up to the gate and sat waiting for the other student to arrive. When his flight was announced over the loud speaker, I hugged Jason and told him to enjoy himself and to call as soon as he got there so I would know that he arrived safely.

I stood at the gate while they boarded the plane and took off. I was relieved yet exhausted. Jason would be safe from the city violence and turmoil during the hot summer.

Each week I glanced uneasily at the calendar and prayed that Jason would be able to complete the entire summer program. The stress had been so great for him that each day away from his world was a great opportunity for him.

Steve Dies

By August, I felt somewhat assured that Jason would finish the entire summer session in Colorado. Yet each day, I was a little on edge. Then one morning as I was eating breakfast and enjoying the beautiful weather, sipping coffee from my favorite cup, I realized that Jason was over the halfway mark. By the seventh week I was feeling just a slight tinge of anxiety. Then the eighth week came and went without incident. There was only one week remaining before he would return to Chicago, but I felt an uneasiness that was unexplainable.

A few days into the ninth week, Mrs. Rainer called with the sad news that Steve had died. "My sympathies are with your family. Jason will be devastated by the news." Mrs. Rainer spoke further, "I don't have the number to reach Jason and we would appreciate it if you would tell Kevin, also." "Mrs. Rainer, I will make sure that Jason is notified right away. Is there anything I can do for your family?" She stated that they were making arrangements and that she would contact me later. "My prayers are with you and your family," I said and hung up. I sat there motionless staring at the telephone.

Memories of the many conversations I had had with Steve about the boys at the group home and the scene at the hospital were running through my mind. This was another major loss for Jason. How much more heartache could he bear? What could I say to soften the blow and comfort him? I sat on the edge of my chair. It was a call that I dreaded.

Jason: Ward of the State

I spoke with Kevin first. It was easy to reach him. He was shocked and sad about Steve's death and concerned about the impact on Jason. I helped Kevin make the necessary arrangements to come home to attend the funeral.

After thumbing through pages of materials for a contact number, I looked at the calendar. Jason had almost made it through the entire summer and had been able to enjoy it without interruption. I was uneasy now knowing that I had to deliver this news.

The phone was frozen in my hand as I looked down at the phone number and forced myself to dial the digits. I spoke with the receptionist who was very pleasant and helpful. "Could you please connect me to Jason?" She responded promptly to the urgency in my voice. "He is out working on the grounds and unable to come to the phone at this time. However, I will notify his superior that it is important for him to contact you as soon as possible." I don't remember saying "Thank you," but I knew it was understood. Within fifteen minutes the phone rang. "It's Jason, how are you doing? Is everything alright?" I tried to remain calm and chose my words carefully. "Jason, Steve has died and his family wanted me to contact you. Do you want to come home to attend his funeral?" Jason was quiet. This devastating news was sinking in. Then he blurted out bits and pieces about Steve and how much he cared about him and Eddie. "Steve cared a lot about you, also. You did a wonderful job of taking care of him. His family also appreciated all of the work that you did to help him through his illness." He seemed to be listening intently. "Do you want me to make arrangements for you to come home as soon as possible?" "Yes." I ended the conversation with "I'll see you later and I'll pick you up at the airport." Jason gained enough composure to say, "I'll see you Mrs. Peterson. Thanks for calling me."

Two days before his Colorado trip was to end, Jason returned home. I had a few errands to run before picking him up at the airport. He was taking a late night flight so I had the whole day to reflect on how much help Steve had given Jason and in turn how much help Jason had given him. The caretaker had become the caregiver. Steve had become more than the liaison between home and school. He had been a true friend and confidant. Jason will probably go through a long period of adjustment, I thought.

I arrived at the airport twenty minutes early so I wouldn't have to rush. I verified the flight number and arrival time. The terminal was almost empty, which was great. A friend had driven with me and upon asking for permission to go to the gate I was told that it wasn't a problem at all because of the scarcity of travelers at this time of night. However, I needed to get a special pass and only one person would be granted that permission. My friend waited in the terminal area.

I walked down the corridor accompanied by the swishing sounds of men and machinery waxing the floors. One or two stragglers were walking around. I finally arrived at the gate. No one was there, not even an attendant. All the seats were empty. No TV monitors were on. The area was very quiet.

The plane taxied up and an elderly couple exited first, followed by a few single passengers with small children. I stepped closer to the door. After a few more moments, I saw Jason coming up the gangway. He was carrying the heavy duffel bag on his back and he looked very tired. He had a deep golden tan and he wore his cap backwards. Jason looked around slowly and saw me standing there waiting to meet him. "Jason!" I called, hoping to break his melancholy mood. "How was your flight?" He perked up a little as I reached out to hug him. There was a faint smile on his face, which made me glad. We walked with the other passengers into the terminal area where my friend greeted Jason and then we headed for the parking lot.

When we reached the car Jason threw his duffel bag into the trunk, opened the back door and got in. He breathed a sigh of relief. We drove in silence. After a few miles, I glanced back at him. He was in deep thought.

Jason: Ward of the State

I remember thinking that maybe Jason could come live with me. I didn't know if it would work, but I had to give him options. I didn't want him to worry about finding another place to live.

Finally, Jason spoke, "I am worried about Eddie. What's going to happen to my friend, Eddie?" I wished I had an answer. "Jason, I really don't know." Eddie was Jason's true friend and confident. Eddie seemed to need Jason more than Jason needed him. They played basketball together and shared many experiences. They trusted each other. I had found out that during the period when Steve was bed ridden, Jason and Eddie went shopping for him, cooked his food, took him to the hospital, washed his clothes and kept his home clean.

I had to give Jason the time, space and support he needed to get through this crisis. He looked at me with such a sad expression. It didn't seem fair that so much was thrust upon his young shoulders. But Jason was a survivor, more mature than his years. He would find a way or a way would find him.

Steve's funeral was on a Friday. Having the services at the end of the week prolonged the agony for Jason. The family had to contact relatives in various locations around the country. I knew firsthand how difficult it is to make preparations for someone's death, let alone endure the progression from anger, frustration and disbelief to acceptance and finality.

Jason had to experience the stages of grief on his own terms, yet I was tenacious in my resolve to help him get through this bereavement period. I remember saying, "Time will heal all wounds." Jason couldn't comprehend this.

The day before the funeral I had taken some food over to Steve's parents' home. They very graciously greeted me at the door and welcomed me into their home. I sat down on a sofa near the front entrance. Several relatives were standing, sitting or walking around the large living room, talking fondly about Steve and sharing special moments.

The next day, funeral services were held at a neighborhood church on the west side where Steve grew up, lived and went to school. It was a large, sturdy gray stone church with a tall steeple. People were milling around outside when I arrived. Some were visibly shaken. Others appeared to be business associates and colleagues. I walked into the church slowly. Soft music was being played on an old pipe organ on the right side of the altar. Scores of people were sitting in the pews and many were moving about, consoling relatives and the immediate family.

I scanned the church looking for Kevin and Jason. They were sitting towards the front. I was so relieved that Kevin and his friend had driven Jason to the funeral. The two boys needed each other more than ever and I didn't want to interfere.

I approached the pew where the boys were sitting and sat as close to them as I could, speaking to them softly as I made my way to my seat. Jason looked up briefly. His eyes were swollen and tears had stained his face. He was sitting next to Eddie and Ashley. Jason was too distressed to respond but Kevin did smile and nod appreciatively.

I read the program and began thinking about something I had just learned. It was Steve who had put Jason and Kevin together in the same group home. He had found out that the brothers had been separated and took a personal interest in their welfare. Also, after Kevin left for college and Jason left the group home, Steve, who had resigned from the group home, intervened again to provide shelter for Jason and Eddie. He took them into his home and became a constant, stable figure in their lives.

The service started with a prayer and scripture reading. There were muffled sounds of grief. I closed my eyes and thought of all my phone calls with Steve about the boys. He

Jason: Ward of the State

had made it possible for me to help them. I felt a sense of obligation to him. He had done so much.

Several ministers spoke about Steve's gift for helping others, especially children. Many others gave personal tributes, sharing with all of us how much Steve had influenced their lives.

After this there was a musical selection. Then the minister surveyed the audience and asked if there were any more acknowledgements. I rose from my seat and nervously made my way to the podium. I had never spoken at a funeral before. It felt as though all eyes were glued on me as I walked up to the microphone and looked directly at Jason and Eddie for a moment to collect my thoughts. "Steve dedicated his life to helping children succeed. His love and compassion for helping others was evident in so many ways." I hesitated a few moments. "Steve knew that education was the key to a bright and promising future. He wanted most of all for Jason and Eddie to get a good education and succeed in life no matter what obstacles were in their way. To honor his memory and the principles that he stood for, I know he wants you to stay in school and stay on the right path." I looked at them and knew that Jason and Eddie had taken in what I said. I heard a few people say "amen" as I returned to my seat behind the brothers. Kevin turned around and waited until I sat down. He seemed happy that I had spoken on his behalf and Jason's.

Another week went by and I received a call from Mrs. Rainer. She wanted to inform me that Jason and Eddie were living in Steve's apartment alone. The Raniers lived just four doors from the apartment, so it was easy to keep tabs on what was happening, but the thought of the boys living there alone was disturbing. Mrs. Rainer and I discussed the pros and cons of the boys living independently and agreed that it was unacceptable. There was drug and gang activity in the area which led to safety issues and dangers. Once I had taken Jason and Eddie to get some groceries and as we turned the corner, I saw a group of boys hanging out on the steps next door to Steve's apartment. My gut feeling was that it was just a matter of time before they would make a move on Jason and Eddie. They had to know that the boys were in the apartment alone.

Mrs. Ranier finally said, "I've decided that the boys will have to leave." I agreed.

Jason's Senior Year

Jason entered his senior year—which should be the most rewarding and fulfilling period, full of fun and expectation—but Jason's entire world was falling apart at the seams. He hadn't fully recovered from Steve's death. I knew he needed time to sort things out and come to terms with where and how to live.

Jason knew the importance of school and he was trying to attend, but he was having severe difficulty concentrating on his school work. He had begun to miss classes again.

The requirements for seniors at Cornell Prep were rigid. The principal was placing tremendous pressure on Jason and there were no compromises, particularly regarding attendance. Seniors were allowed to miss a total of eight days during the entire school year and Jason had already missed five.

The pressure was mounting. I could hear it in his voice and it was evident in his actions. He was disinterested and couldn't get his act together.

Over the years, I had forged a friendship with the senior counselor, Mrs. Davison. We had spoken numerous times over the course of Jason's years at Cornell. On this occasion, Mrs. Davison told me very directly, "I'm not saying that you are not doing all that you can, but he requires more service and help than the majority of our students." Those words—the majority of the students—echoed in my head.

Jason: Ward of the State

Jason couldn't be put with the majority of anything. His life and situation were far more severe than that of the other students, I thought. Yet the rules and regulations were set. There could be no accommodations or modifications for one student without making allowances for all the others. As an educator I could see the need for these rules, yet I found it hard to accept them under the circumstances.

I had even sent a floral arrangement to the principal, hoping that she would soften her stance toward Jason, but to no avail. She thanked me for the beautiful flowers but didn't leave any room at all for further discussion. I had done everything in my power to keep Jason in school but he was still missing days. Feeling a little despondent myself, I looked out the window, wondering where he was and what he was doing. I had almost reached the end of my rope.

Then as I was preparing supper, the phone rang. It was Mrs. Larkins, the principal at Cornell Prep. "Hello, Mrs. Peterson, I would like to have a meeting with you and Jason tomorrow morning. Would you be able to attend at 10:00 a.m.?" I was stunned. I thought that I had exhausted every avenue at Cornell. "Yes, I would be glad to meet with you, Mrs. Larkins," I said, and asked if she would be able to contact Jason. She said, "Yes." The next morning, I met Jason outside the principal's office. After a few minutes, the secretary ushered us in. "Mrs. Peterson, how nice to see you again. Jason, how are you doing?" Jason smiled. We sat in front of her massive oak desk.

Mrs. Larkins looked at us through her thick glasses. I could tell by her demeanor that it wasn't going to be a friendly meeting. She spoke first, looking directly at Jason. "I was wondering, young man, why you have been absent so many times from school. Your attendance record is not very good." Jason was fidgeting. He looked over at me as if we shared a secret. I understood and acknowledged the pleading glance in my direction. Then Jason turned, looked at Mrs. Larkins and meekly responded, "School doesn't matter when you have no place to live."

His statement was barely audible, yet I heard every word loud and clear. I was shocked at his blunt revelation. Mrs. Larkins's expression didn't change. It was as if she had not heard him make a totally honest statement from his innermost soul. "Jason doesn't have a place to live, Mrs. Larkins. That is one of the reasons that he has missed so much school." Again she didn't respond.

I knew in my heart that the principal liked Jason. She had spoken to me often about his polite manner and the potential she saw in him. That was probably one of the reasons she had allowed him to repeat his first year. Without her consent, he would have had to transfer to another school. I realized now that she had exhausted all of her options; however, she had decided to meet one more time to listen to his concerns. I couldn't imagine Jason not graduating from Cornell Prep.

I had never heard Jason complain about his life or the hand he had been dealt. To me, he was trying to live his life as best he could. At the meeting, Mrs. Larkins had him sign a contract stating that he could only be absent one more half day. She was asking him to make a promise that he knew was impossible to keep. His head was down and he rocked back and forth in his chair. For a moment, I sat there speechless looking at the principal, trying to digest what had taken place. Yet, a small voice was telling me that we could move forward in spite of the setbacks, in spite of the needs.

Mrs. Larkins excused us rather abruptly. She was not sympathetic nor was she very understanding. I couldn't imagine anyone being so curt in light of Jason's problems. She dismissed his situation as if it really didn't matter one way or the other.

I offered to drive Jason home. What I had not known before the meeting was that Mrs. Rainer had given the boys an ultimatum to be out of the apartment by a certain date.

Jason: Ward of the State

We sat in the car and I looked over at Jason. His spirits were crushed. "I couldn't believe that Mrs. Larkins didn't understand your situation," I said after a long silence. Jason slumped down in his seat and stared out the window. "Perhaps, if she knew all the problems and issues that you are facing, she might allow you to remain at Cornell Prep." Jason was still staring straight ahead at the growing traffic. We both knew the truth. The chapter at Cornell Prep was now closed.

I received a confirming letter in the mail. It was devastating for him and me because all of my efforts to keep him in school had failed. I was feeling desperate, hindered by a lack of options. But I vowed that this distraction would not keep me from seeing the bigger picture of Jason completing his senior year and graduating. I kept my hopes high and my expectations constant.

In the course of one of our conversations I had asked Jason if he would consider getting a GED. "I don't ever want to get a GED. I want to finish high school and graduate like everyone else," he said. A flicker of hope was lit and my job was to keep it burning.

Another week went by. I had no word from Jason and no way of reaching him. I feared for his safety and well being. More days passed. My fears were mounting. I wondered if Jason had lost all hope of going back to school or living in general. I got ready for bed early. The sun was just sinking below a ribbon of gray clouds.

The next morning, I woke up from a restless sleep and prepared a simple breakfast of toast and coffee. As I sat down to eat, the telephone rang and startled me. I reached over the counter to answer it. It was Jason. I didn't hesitate to ask how he was doing and where he was living, but Jason didn't allow me to say anything further.

"Mrs. Peterson, can I come and live with you and go to school?" I was surprised but kept my voice calm and steady. I didn't hesitate to say "Yes." Over the past seven years, I had been in Jason's life, but only indirectly. Now we were taking a giant step together. We had developed a bond of trust and support, but in my mind, I had been connected to him only by a thread. Would this living arrangement work? Jason was still in the welfare system and there were countless hurdles to cross before I could act on his request.

Becoming a Legal Guardian

I had to think fast. I told Jason that I would have to call the DCFS, the Department of Children and Family Service to speak to his social worker. As far as the "System" was concerned, Jason was probably considered lost. He was still in the record books because of his age, but no one had heard from him in quiet some time.

The receptionist at DCFS said, "Mr. Slone doesn't work here anymore." Then I asked to speak with Mrs. Anderson. I was searching my mind frantically for a familiar name.

I remembered my first experience with Jason's social worker. I had called and made an appointment, then went to the office to meet her. I poured out my heart and soul trying to let the social worker know that she had my full cooperation in helping Jason make it in the "System." There were many social workers on Jason's case over a period of time. I thought about how hard it must be for children to encounter new faces on a constant basis.

As I was searching my mind for a familiar name, the receptionist asked the name of the child. "Please wait a moment," she said. When she returned she gave me the name of his current case worker, Mr. Samuels.

Moments later Mr. Samuels was on the phone. Once I identified myself and my relationship to Jason he seemed eager to help me get Jason back in school. "Mrs. Peterson, I have been reviewing our records on Jason Jefferson and I am amazed at your active role in his life." I was very happy to

Jason: Ward of the State

be recognized but the main purpose of our conversation was to discuss Jason and how we could get him back into school.

Mr. Samuels reviewed Jason's records some more then said that he wanted to meet me so that we could go over some forms and research any options. "I will be happy to meet with you, Mr. Samuels," I said. He asked the receptionist to schedule a meeting for Thursday morning. We agreed on 10:30 a.m. Mr. Samuels had mentioned that other DCFS staff and his supervisor, Mrs. Cummings, would be in attendance. I looked forward to the meeting.

Thursday morning came. I was a little apprehensive at first but I had to be an effective advocate for Jason. We had come too far together.

I arrived at DCFS, signed in, and Mr. Samuels led me into the meeting. I was welcomed by the educational coordinator and seconds later, his supervisor came into the room. After introductions, Mr. Samuels reviewed the guidelines for children in the welfare system, along with age limits and official papers. I mentioned that Jason had asked to live with me so that he could attend school. Mr. Samuels spoke first. "Mrs. Peterson, Jason is now 18 years old, going on 19. He has had your support over the years. So many of our youth need people like you to get involved." "I only wanted to do what was best for Jason," I said. Everyone at the table smiled.

Mr. Samuels went on. "We heard that Jason had been living with Steve Rainer until he died and now he is in the apartment with his friend, Eddie." I simply answered, "Yes. Mrs. Rainer, Steve's mother, told me that the boys are still living in Steve's old apartment without adult supervision. We have been in contact since Steve's death and the issue of the boys being in his home alone is disturbing for both of us." Everyone looked surprised that the boys had been able to manage for such a long time on their own. Mr. Samuels stated that, "The boys could live independently with the agency's help on the side. It is called independent living. They would be able to manage their allotment, housing,

Jason: Ward of the State

food, school and transportation needs." I was appalled at that suggestion. "No," I said. "Jason, especially, is not ready for an independent living arrangement. He has had too many obstacles and traumas in his life and still needs adult supervision and direction. I am totally against that type of arrangement. Perhaps it works for some children, but I have my reservations about the program as it relates to Jason."

Mr. Samuels was very pensive during our discussion and made comments on which type of school would best suit him, suggesting that Jason get a GED. He made strong statements about Jason not being interested in school and maybe needing placement in another group home. I couldn't believe what I was hearing. Another group home would make him regress even further. I strongly opposed that suggestion because Jason would become even more lost and confused with rules and regulation that would stifle his growth and development.

I was also vehemently opposed to him living alone and being pushed into adulthood before he was ready. I looked sternly at each individual before me. I had to struggle to make my point strong and clear. Finally, after an hour or more, Mr. Samuels asked, "Are you willing and able to be Jason's guardian, Mrs. Peterson, and accept all of the responsibilities that go with it?" I glanced around the room one more time. I couldn't believe that I had gotten so emotionally upset over the lack of options for children like Jason and how little they knew about his real character and abilities. Knowing that Jason would be floundering without direct support, I agreed to accept the position of guardianship. The room became very still and quiet. All eyes were cast on me as I made the commitment to be Jason's legal guardian.

Mr. Samuels stated that Jason would have to agree to reside in an Approved Self-Selected Placement, pursuant to DCFS policy and procedure. This was Jason's choice. Mr. Samuels then went through the legal documents with me and stated that the papers would be filed. I was willing to go through all of the proceedings and anything necessary to assure that Jason's case be handled in the right way. Mr. Samuels stated that the educational coordinator would be more than happy to assist in getting Jason into school. I quickly acknowledge that we would appreciate her help. Everything had progressed favorably in Jason's direction for guardianship. I was overjoyed. I went home feeling upbeat and exhilarated.

Jason Comes Home

The following week I was preparing my heart and home for Jason. I had no experience with child rearing. I had numerous nieces and nephews, but Jason was special and I was eager to welcome him into my home. I thought about the major changes and adjustments I would have to make to be his guardian. First, I knew that I wanted to be home to supervise his comings and goings. My mother was always home when we prepared for school in the morning and she was always there when we came home in the afternoon. This was my main focus.

Then, I went into the guest bedroom. There would have to be some major changes in the furniture and décor. Jason would certainly need a computer to do his homework. I mentally arranged the room as I thought about new curtains and a throw rug. He needed a desk for studying and a good lamp for reading. He was nineteen years old now and college and adulthood were staring him in the face.

A day later, the case worker called with information about the services that Jason may need to support his new family-orientated environment. I had to update him on Jason's school records and difficulties. I'm sure it is problematic to handle so many cases, yet Mr. Samuels appeared competent and professional. He was a very delightful person but it was

Jason: Ward of the State

difficult at first to gain his confidence. But it was worth the effort to adjust to new people, just as Jason and other children were continually forced to do. He was delighted that the process was moving smoothly and that there were no obstacles hindering the guardianship.

I expected my life as I knew it to be on hold until Jason graduated from high school. Was I totally aware of what I was getting into? Did my hopes and dreams for Jason cloud my view of reality? Was this going to work? I wondered if Jason had become so independent, living at Steve's house where he could come and go as he pleased, that he wouldn't be able to adjust to a more structured living environment with me as his guardian. Jason hadn't lived in a structured family environment since becoming a ward of the state seven years ago. This was going to be a new experience for both of us.

The next day I drove to the west side to pick up Jason and his belongings. He still appeared very depressed and despondent about Steve's death and the uncertainty of his future. I told him that everything was going to work out fine and not to worry. Jason turned slightly and managed a faint smile.

We arrived home and I introduced him to his room and told him where everything was. I had a few ground rules about being home before curfew during the week. Jason seemed pleased. "Tomorrow, we will look into getting you back in school," I said, having no idea that it was going to be a huge ordeal because of the circumstances under which he left Cornell Prep. Because he was a senior Jason needed to catch up on course credits in order to graduate.

The next day with the help of the case worker and the local educational director for DCFS, we set off to enroll Jason in another private high school. We were not prepared for the stonewalling we received from the administration there. The counselor wasn't too sure if Jason was a good candidate for the school. He told Jason that he needed to cut his hair, so we did that immediately. That evening I called some

Jason: Ward of the State

prominent people in the community and asked them to contact the school on Jason's behalf because we were having such a hard time getting him admitted. They agreed to call, but there was no response from the school. I made many attempts to reach the principal, with no success. A whole week went by. I could see frustration and disappointment beginning to set in. Jason was just waiting, getting nowhere. Finally, I suggested that perhaps a public school would solve our problems and he agreed. It was walking distance from our home.

Jason set his alarm clock for 7:00 a.m. We ate breakfast and then planned our day. The case worker and educational director for DCFS agreed to meet us at the public school just in case any problems occurred. We went to the office and the clerk gave us the necessary enrollment forms. Jason took the time to fill them out and get other information about the school's rules and regulations. The students didn't have to wear uniforms but they had to look presentable and neat every day.

After registering in the office, we walked down another corridor to see the counselor. Jason was getting excited about his new school. He was looking at the trophy cases in the hallway and the racially mixed group of students. We passed the security guard near the front door. I knew this woman right away. She was Mrs. Dixon and had once been a preschool teacher's aide at my school. I introduced her to Jason. "He's starting his senior year here and I would appreciate it if you would look out for him." Mrs. Dixon smiled. "It's good to meet you, young man. Don't worry about him at all, Mrs. Peterson. He'll be in good hands." I thanked her. When we entered the counselor's office, I immediately recognized Dr. Watson. His family had owned and operated the local cleaners in the neighborhood in which I grew up. It was wonderful to see another familiar face. He assured me that he would personally make sure that Jason was assigned all of the courses needed for him to graduate in June and would periodically check his progress. He also told Jason that he would have to take two evening classes to make up some of his requirements. I heard Jason assure Dr. Watson that he would do whatever was required to graduate in June.

We learned that seniors had been assigned a counselor to assist them with college applications and information. Jason was going to have to work hard to catch up because school had already been in session for over two weeks. The case worker and educational director were amazed at how Jason worked with Dr. Watson to complete his registration for courses. Once that was done, we stopped at a restaurant to have lunch. We were now on the right road and the path was clear. We even shopped for that special book bag that would hold all of his books and supplies.

On his first day at Lincoln High, Jason walked to class and even came home for lunch. I thought that I would have the entire day free until he came home in the afternoon, but right at 11:30 a.m. he walked through the door, ready for lunch. In fact, he made it a regular habit to come home for lunch. Things were working well with the school and home arrangement so far. I was still apprehensive and anxious about my skills as a guardian but with each day a routine was being established and we were adjusting to each other's habits. I made it clear that I wanted to give Jason his space and freedom to adapt to his new situation. He would come home from school at about 3:00 p.m., take a short nap, fix something to eat then retreat to his room to do his homework. He did this until his evening classes started. Eventually, Jason was revealing more and more about his feelings and things that were bothering him. On a regular basis, I would ask him about school and we were really getting to know each other. We shared dinner and conversations, which made the evenings enjoyable. He even cleaned up after himself and washed his own dishes.

I found out quickly that he was a great cook. He liked to prepare simple dishes but was willing to try new recipes. I provided the groceries he needed to prepare dinner and other meals. One of my conversations starters was, "What are you cooking today that smells so good?" Between the group home and taking care of Steve, Jason had learned many survival lessons that gave him a certain level of competence and skill. It didn't take long to get used to the smell of fried chicken, pork chops sizzling on the stove or beef or turkey roast.

Sometimes Jason would visit Eddie, who was living with an aunt. He would spend the weekends with him, mindful of the fact that he had to return at a decent hour on Sunday to get ready for school. They were still friends and he wanted to keep that friendship strong.

Lincoln High

At his new high school, Jason realized that he had missed a lot of instruction in key subject areas and needed help. I couldn't believe that he asked for tutoring himself. He was also working several jobs at school to fulfill his community service credits.

One Wednesday morning while I was busy enjoying the freedom of a quiet house I received a telephone call from Jason. He said that he needed updated medical shots. I immediately said that I would take him to get them, even though a few days earlier I had just taken him to get a complete physical examination. Fifteen minutes later, he was home and we left for the medical center only to find out that his records showed that he had already taken the shots. I took him back to school. The officer acknowledged that he had made a mistake. I waved "good-bye" and headed home.

Thirty minutes later Jason was back for lunch. I heard his keys jingling in the keyhole and the brief silence I had was now over. "I'll make you two chicken meltdown sandwiches," I said quickly as he barged into the kitchen. Without waiting for an answer, I made the sandwiches and watched him devour one of them. My mother used to make these special sandwiches when I was a little girl. She would fry strips of chicken in a large skillet and when the meat was almost done, she would add a piece of cheese and let it melt down around the edges before she placed the entire thing between slices of bread. I loved watching her make these sandwiches because they were so thick and satisfying. As I was making the other sandwich and placing it on a plate, Jason got up from his seat and started looking around the house for something. I asked, "What are you looking for, Jason?" He was still searching around the doorway and front hallway when he said, "I can't find my ID card." I helped him look, but we couldn't find it. He thought that perhaps he'd dropped it in the car. I grabbed my hat and coat and we searched the car thoroughly inside and out without finding the ID card. I said, "It's raining now so I'll drive you back to school." We drove about a block when I realized that I did not have my purse, so I turned the corner and told Jason that he was going to have to walk back to school because I didn't have my driver's license.

At home I tried to resume my activities and to have a little peace and quiet. In a few hours, Jason's key was turning the lock in the door. Was this a sample of what my life was going to be? I was tired and worn out with the day's activities yet I felt fulfilled and happy. Parenting wasn't going to be easy, but I had to get used to it. That night, I went to bed relieved that the day was done.

Entering Lincoln High as a senior had its own challenges and obstacles but to my utter surprise, Jason settled into his role as student and I settled into my role as parent. Sometimes I would start a conversation by asking him, "What are some of the assignments you have to do for your history and English classes?" Jason would respond with simple, direct answers such as, "I have to do several research papers and there is a mid-term and final exam." Other times, I would get bits and pieces about certain instructors he liked and how demanding some of his classes were. Jason was totally focused on school and he appeared happy and content. He had joined several school organizations and was participating in a mock United Nations Conference and planning a trip to Springfield with a selected group of students. For me, everything was falling into place. Jason was moving in the right direction and it wasn't taking as much effort as I had expected.

At home, I felt comfortable providing Jason with a quiet learning environment, a stable living arrangement and as much freedom as possible. Finishing his senior year was an important objective and I was happy to help Jason become independent so that he could take care of himself in the future.

Soon it was time for Report Card pick-up. I braced myself even though I knew that the situation was far better than it had been in the past. Jason came home after school and handed me the note announcing the date and time for parents and guardians to meet with teachers. The note stated that the meeting with each instructor should last no more then fifteen minutes. I asked Jason if he wanted to accompany me. His face lit up. For the first time in years, Jason was enthusiastic about his grades.

We entered the front door of Lincoln High where the floors and windows had been polished to perfection. The school smelled fresh and clean. Colorful bulletin boards and decorations and posters welcomed the parents to the campus. Jason walked a few steps ahead of me. He was eager to have me meet his teachers and get reports on his progress. There was a bounce to his step that hadn't been there before. I couldn't help myself. I smiled broadly and was thrilled to be his official guardian.

Jason: Ward of the State

A security guard recognized Jason immediately and he introduced himself to me. "Hello, I'm Mr. Rogers. Jason is a fine young man. You must be his mother." I felt the blood rushing up to my face as I blushed at the mention of being his biological mother. Without divulging too much information, I smiled warmly and nodded. "You are Mr. Rogers? Jason has mentioned you many times at home. Thanks for taking an interest in him." Mr. Rogers stated further that "Jason is a nice student. You can tell he has good home training." Jason was beaming. Little did Mr. Rogers know the full extent of his remarks but the compliment was well taken. We were anxious to meet his teachers. I waved good-bye as Jason shook Mr. Rogers' hand. We walked in the direction of the classrooms. On our way, a group of parents and students seated at a table handed us a parent guide book and a map of the school and room numbers.

We went to meet his math teacher, Mrs. Grimes, in room 204. Mrs. Grimes was a very personable teacher. She greeted Jason and me warmly. Jason introduced us and she began to rave about his performance. "Jason has made considerable progress in my class. He works really hard and is doing quite well." Jason stood there beaming with pride. Mrs. Grimes showed me her grade book and pointed out Jason's great grades. I couldn't believe the 80s, 90s and 100s. He had even done extra math assignments to improve his grades.

We left and went to his other classes. Each teacher gave a glowing account of Jason's progress. All of them spoke highly of him and admired his determination to catch up. The majority of the grades were As and Bs. He was proud as a peacock.

I was elated about the change that had taken place. I always knew he had the potential to do great things and become a success in life. He just needed a new focus, direction and stability. My doubts and fears were melting away. I knew now that Jason was motivated and prepared to do anything necessary to guarantee his progress and graduation.

Jason's Story

When he returned home from one of his evening classes, I could tell that Jason had something on his mind. He didn't retreat to his room right after eating. "Mrs. Peterson, I was thinking about applying to some colleges. Some of my friends at school are applying to colleges and I better start getting the applications filled out." I was thrilled to see that things were turning around for him and he was ready to make some serious decisions. "Jason, I would love to help you apply. We have to get the college catalogues and look through them to see what courses they offer in the area you want to major in." He was looking at me intently as I mentioned the steps for applying and getting accepted at a good school. Jason wasn't sure about which schools to apply to at first, so we just spoke generally about where some of his friends wanted to go and what course of study he wanted to pursue. I also mentioned that he would need to speak to his school counselor about financial aid and specific colleges in the area.

Jason was in an up-beat mood for several days after our conversation. He began sending off for college catalogues and getting information from his counselor at school. In a few days the dining room table had turned into a college recruitment center with brochures, applications, pictures, and articles about different colleges. The names of many of the colleges that we were researching were new to me. We took time to look up schools in the Chicago area first then we branched off into neighboring states.

Jason was on a mission and so was I. The only thing holding back our progress was Jason's grades and school records. He looked slightly defeated when I mentioned that "grades, classroom performance, attendance and scores are vital to getting into college, but sometimes a personal message in the form of a cover letter can make a world of difference in getting into the school of your choice." Jason started to pace back and forth in the living room. I didn't want him to lose faith; I didn't want him to give up.

Then I remembered that my sister, Connie, and I had helped Kevin write a cover letter to go with his applications. "Why do I need a cover letter?" Jason asked inquisitively. "Jason, a college gets numerous applications from students all over the nation and abroad. Some students are selected and some aren't. When you send a personal cover letter to introduce yourself, your application might stand out from the others." Jason stopped pacing. I was thinking about the difficult and complicated life he had lived so far. He had been through so much just to survive on a daily basis. "An application doesn't reveal the whole person," I finally said. "It is sometimes good to let a school know that you are an individual, not a number."

He understood what I was saying and his mood brightened. He realized that his particular situation was unlike other students', yet he had special gifts and abilities that made him a stronger candidate for college.

I got up to locate the letter so Jason could see what we had written for Kevin. I looked in the back of the second drawer of my desk where I keep important papers and there was the treasured letter. I handed it over to Jason to read. He looked at me and closed his eyes for a moment then looked back at the letter holding it tightly. Jason walked over to the other side of the room then he went into his bedroom so he could read it in private.

I left the room also to give him some space and allow him to digest the contents. Jason was in his room for quite a while. I busied myself by folding some laundry. I wanted him

Jason: Ward of the State

to take as much time as necessary to think about his experiences and be able to express them in a letter.

After about fifteen minutes, Jason emerged. I thought he had Kevin's cover letter still in his hand, but he gave me a different document. It appeared to be a term paper or essay. "Mrs. Peterson, I want you to read this paper. I wrote it when I was a junior at Cornell Prep." I braced myself. He walked to the other side of the room, his head down, his face drawn, his eyes becoming dark.

The paper drew me like a magnet. I had to read it to find out what made him become distant and withdrawn so suddenly.

The title of the paper was "Life and Its Ups and Downs." This simple title had deep, far reaching meaning and purpose. He had written:

"Life is a state of being and everyone thinks that they can get through life by trying to avoid bad things that might come their way as they find their purpose in life. The only way I really can speak on such an issue is if I use the facts that I have experienced in my own life. The point I'm trying to make is that the problems in this world are basically unavoidable and everyone, no matter how great or small will have to face them."

He went on: "When I was just five years old, I used to have to stand outside in the cold with my brother while my mother begged for money from strangers. I could tell that something was wrong with my mother. At the time, I didn't understand what mental illness was or how it would affect a family. But when I got older, I started to wonder why we were begging for money for something to eat when we had food at the crib. This was a serious situation at the time, one I didn't fully understand.

"During this time my brother and I were living across town with our mother. My father would come and check on us at my mother's house. Then in 1990, because of her illness, it was apparent we had to leave and go live with my father on the east side of Chicago. My parents grew up together and even lived next door to each other. When my mother was released from the hospital she returned to live with her mother, our grandmother, in one house and right next door, my father was living with his parents. In other words, we had two sets of grandparents living next door to each other. This made life easy and difficult. We were shifted back and forth between the two houses.

"Time was our enemy when my mother was in and out of the hospital. Each time she left and returned from the hospital, we felt abandoned and alone. We thought that life would get better because now we lived with our father while our mother was in the hospital getting well. We were enrolled at the neighborhood public school and we were excited about starting a new life and adventure. We used to go over to see our mother every day. She appeared to be doing better. But our grandmother was never nice to us. Each time we came over to visit, she would tell us to go straight to the basement and be silent. If we didn't abide by her rules, she would send us back next door. We were kids and it was almost impossible to stay quiet very long so we were sent home every day. School wasn't as great as we thought it would be either. I got into a fight every other day. I was suspended often from school. I would always take up for my brother and would even fight for him because I thought that's what real brothers do.

"In June of 1995 my brother and I were playing in our room and I hit him in the head and he started crying. My father was furious; he told us that if we didn't keep down the noise that he was going to punish us. Then he came into the room and gave us a whooping. He accidentally hit me across my face and left a mark. When my father left to go to work, I went next door to my mother's house and told her what happened. She was upset about the mark on my head and she called the police and pressed charges against him. When the courts and police report checked into my

Jason: Ward of the State

mother's background and found out that she had a history of mental illness, they determined that she was not fit to take care of us so my brother and I were sent to live in a group home. My mother constantly tried to get us back over a period of two years but all of her efforts failed.

"The following years were very stormy for me. Then in 1998, I would enter my first year of high school at Cornell Prep with the help of my former teacher, Mrs. Peterson. I saw nothing but a future of opportunity and success. I didn't know that I would blow the first year of high school because of the many distractions outside of school and my home situation. The following year I came back and was determined not to fail again. With the help of my teachers and peers, I was able to stay at Cornell Prep and I actually did well in school. I am now entering my junior year and my life still is an up and down roller coaster, yet I beat the odds and made it. I have reconciled with my father and I see him often. My mother is still ill and I rarely visit her. As for me, I am still attending Cornell Prep and I plan on attending college afterwards. I am looking forward to pursuing a law degree. I wish my story could in some way inspire other young boys who are going through similar problems to have faith in God and never think you have lost until the race is over."

I read this paper over and over, thinking to myself how, in the blink of an eye, Jason's and Kevin's lives were changed forever. I was amazed. I closed my eyes and remembered seeing Jason in my first grade class. I knew so little about him at the time. I recalled the story he wrote that had had such a profound effect on my teaching ever after.

This was the first time that I had the total picture of what really happened to the boys, how Jason and Kevin became wards of the state and the circumstances that permanently shaped their lives. I reflected on the day that I went to court and the judge was about to give the boys back to their mother. We will never know how they would have fared if the decision had been made for them to return to their mother.

The numerous twists and turns in life are sometimes astonishing.

Jason's Day

The Thanksgiving holiday was rapidly approaching. Jason usually spent this day with my family, but this particular Thanksgiving celebration held a special significance. Jason asked if he could invite some of his closest friends to share the holiday with us. He wanted his good friend, Ashley, along with Eddie and three other friends from school to join us.

The air was filled with excitement because this time he was organizing everything himself. This was going to be "Jason's Day."

We sat down at the dining room table one evening to work out all the details. We agreed on having the traditional Thanksgiving dinner with all of the trimmings. I especially enjoyed baking two apple pies, one peach cobbler and several cakes on Thanksgiving, so those were on the list.

We were in a joyful mood cleaning the house, buying and preparing the food and arranging the table. We got the crystal out and polished that along with the silver, and retrieved the good china. Everything had to be perfect for this special celebration. Jason contacted each of his friends on the telephone and asked them to arrive at 4:00 p.m. He was totally in charge of the day and I couldn't help admiring his leadership abilities and skills.

Everyone arrived on time. Jason greeted each friend at the door and ushered them into the living room. Ashley arrived first. Jason had met Ashley at Cornell Prep at the beginning of his junior year. I had seen her many times at school and she was always friendly and sincere, though very quiet. Jason mentioned how smart she was and that she wanted to go to college. Ashley greeted me cordially and took a seat. "It's so nice to see you again," she said. "What

Jason: Ward of the State

have you been doing lately?" Ashley was beaming proudly. "I have been accepted at Brown University where I will be majoring in biological science." I always knew that Ashley would be a success in life.

The door bell rang again. Jason answered and hugged his friend, Eddie. Eddie waved in my direction and said, "Hi." He stood in the vestibule a few moments before joining Ashley in the living room. His face was aglow. Minutes later, Jason's three other friends arrived. There was Joseph, whom he had met during his junior year at Cornell Prep. He was a tall lanky lad with light brown hair and greenish gray eyes. He was also on the basketball team. Darnell and Lawrence had arrived with him. I didn't know them but noted that Jason had chosen his friends well. They were all nice, well mannered young people who were respectful and supportive of his circumstances and plight.

It was heading toward 4:45 p.m. when Jason announced that dinner was about to be served. He directed everyone to where they would sit. He wanted to be at the end of the table across from Ashley. Dinner was set up buffet style so that they could serve themselves. I heard someone ask, "Who's going to bless the table?" I was standing in the kitchen doorway when all eyes looked in Eddie's direction. Without hesitation, Eddie gave the most eloquent and endearing prayer I had ever heard. "I want to thank God for this wonderful time to share Thanksgiving dinner with my friends. I am glad that I have good friends to share and care about me." There was a joint "Amen" then they dove into the tasty feast. I served my plate and retreated to the den to eat and rest.

It was so good to see Jason happy and animated in conversation. He made sure that everyone was taken care of and felt comfortable. It appeared that everybody enjoyed the meal because the plates were empty. I thought about how unselfish Jason was in inviting friends who didn't have any place to go for the Thanksgiving holiday. He was really happy to have a home environment to share with the people who meant the most to him. It was truly a day to be thankful and feel blessed.

After dinner everyone helped clear the table and put the leftover food in the refrigerator. Jason did most of the work because he wanted his guests to enjoy themselves and not worry about cleaning up, washing dishes and putting the silverware in its proper place. But the tasks were done more efficiently with more hands so all pitched in and enjoyed each other's company in the process.

Everyone retreated to the living room where Ashley sat down first and the boys followed. It was good that they included Ashley in their lively conversations. She knew a lot about Jason's past and his future plans and objectives.

When the conversation turned to sports, I tuned the radio to a soft music station and busied myself in the kitchen.

At about 9:00 p.m. Jason's friends prepared to leave. Eddie spoke up first. "I have to get up early and interview for a new job. Thank you, Mrs. Peterson. Jason, I'll be in touch with you later." Ashley got up from her place on the sofa. The other three friends declared, "We enjoyed ourselves and hope we can get together again soon." Jason was beaming. His dinner had been a success and everything had gone just as he'd planned it.

The Christmas holiday came and went quickly. In a few days Jason would begin the last semester of his senior year. He was more focused than ever and determined to graduate. The course work was still a problem for him, but he persevered and made good grades. Dozens of letters and college catalogs arrived in the mail each day. It really impressed me that Jason was actually planning for his future and his future involved continuing his education.

In early spring he received a call from his former boss in Colorado asking him to work at the campground that summer. I knew that Jason was hoping to secure that summer position. It was a job he thoroughly enjoyed and

Jason: Ward of the State

this time around Jason seemed more committed to spending the entire ten weeks with the Forest Rangers in the mountains. I breathed a sigh of relief that he would be away from the savage city streets and in an environment with fewer dangers and distractions. He wouldn't be connected with any school-based or sponsored program this time, so he would be working independently. It was an answer to my prayers.

Before I knew it we had to prepare for his prom, senior luncheon and graduation. There was a flurry of activity to meet deadlines, pay fees, shop for outfits and purchase graduation pictures for the family. There were numerous meetings, informative flyers, deadlines, senior rings, yearbooks among other things to consider. Several parents and I decided that we would rent a limousine for the prom so that the young people would be safe. Jason and Ashley agreed that it would be a good idea. They could enjoy themselves and not have to worry about traffic and parking.

I took Jason shopping for that special suit. He tried one on and I noticed that he stood in front of the mirror for was seemed like an extremely long time, just looking at himself. I was off to the side, so he didn't see me. The sales person walked away and just let Jason admire himself in the mirror. I wondered what was going through his head. Was he looking down the road with a law degree in one hand and a brief case in the other? Was he imagining the possibilities of a bright future? We purchased the suit and other items that he needed.

The senior prom finally arrived. I was as excited as he was. Jason left early to pick up Ashley so that I could take pictures. Ashley looked beautiful. Her dress was a light lavender color adorned with soft ribbons and flowers. Her shoulder length hair was swept up and entwined with lavender bows. Soft tendril curls fell lightly around her face. A darker colored wrap draped her shoulders. She wore a corsage and Jason wore a boutonniere. I took pictures. A few members of my family came by to send them off. They were excited, too, to see Jason so dapper and debonair.

Jason took Ashley's hand and escorted her to the door after the picture taking session was over. A few neighbors came to see the couple off and I welcomed them in. Jason was beaming and ready to start the magical evening. I was smiling from the inside out. This was indeed a day to remember and treasure.

Jason Graduates

The prom ended and the next event was the senior luncheon. It was held at a large banquet facility on the south side of Chicago. I accompanied Jason and we had a wonderful time. The program was short but drilled home the message that "graduation is one major step in the right direction." A simple lunch of salad, chicken, baked potato and mixed vegetables was served and there was a nice assortment of desserts which we both enjoyed. Several members of Jason's class recited poetry and bequeathed favorite artifacts and belongings they treasured to the next class.

I recognized several parents and felt proud to be with them. I also thought about Jason's real parents and felt sad that they would miss this special celebration. I couldn't believe that over four years had passed and that Jason was actually graduating. I reminded him that his determination and strength in the face of tremendous obstacles got him to this day. Jason listened intently as I spoke those words. We both knew what those obstacles were and how each one was overcome. I wanted him to be proud of his accomplishments and stand tall.

We received enough graduation tickets for Kevin to attend and I was so glad that Jason's brother could witness this milestone and share in the joy of the occasion.

Jason: Ward of the State

The pianist started playing "Pomp and Circumstance." The march sent chills down my spine. The students were lined up according to height so I knew that Jason would be towards the end. Each graduate walked proudly to the beat of the music and perfectly in step. A few had somber faces but most students couldn't contain their true happiness and exhilaration. I had my video camera ready, recording every minute. Finally, I saw Jason and captured each step as he moved closer and closer to his seat at the front of the auditorium. The class valedictorian and salutatorian took their places on the stage along with the guest speaker, teachers, principal, assistant principal and other staff. The stage was decorated with flowers and banners in the school colors. The auditorium was a sea of caps and gowns and proud parents and family members and friends. The choir performed a few selections before the guest speaker gave his enlightening message to "keep up the good work" and "you are the future leaders of this nation."

After other remarks and speeches, the moment that everyone was waiting for arrived. The principal stepped forward and row by row, the graduates stood to receive their diplomas. Some parents were applauding as their child's name was read while other strained to get a closer glimpse of their graduate. I raised my camera and zoomed in to capture Jason walking across the stage. He turned in our direction as he sauntered across, smiling broadly. Kevin was calling his name. Jason extended one hand to the principal and the other to receive his diploma. It was the most wonderful picture.

The class sang their school song, turned their tassels and marched out of the room as the recessional played in the background. Words can't describe the happiness I felt at that moment. I hugged Jason tightly as Kevin reached over to shake his hand. We took pictures and pictures and more pictures. Jason wanted to go out to dinner to celebrate further. We chose one of his favorite restaurants. We had a great time. It was truly Jason's day.

College

Jason was now officially a candidate for Southern Illinois University. I couldn't believe it when he got his acceptance letter. For weeks he had waited for news from various universities and colleges. Yet Jason was impressed with Southern Illinois. Jason had decided previously to major in history and minor in English. I wasn't surprised because he basically had his mind set on being a lawyer. Jason's grandfather had been a lawyer and he was probably his role model. I didn't know much about his grandfather but I was pleased that a member of his family had made an impact on him. I was also elated that Jason scored well enough to take all college level courses at the university. Now he could pursue his dreams.

Once we were sitting at the dining room table and Jason was in a pensive mood. "I can't wait until school starts," he said. I reminded him that he had never given up hope, no matter how dire the circumstances. He had gone through so much turmoil and turbulence. He deserved to be happy.

"The Life and Times of Jason"

Just before Jason left for college, he gave me a booklet entitled "Senior Memory Book." The subtitle was "The Life and Times of Jason." He told me that it was a required assignment for seniors. He also said that he had been working on it for some time. His teacher had graded his booklet and gave it back to him to keep. Here is an excerpt from Jason's senior year booklet. In it he wrote:

Jason: Ward of the State

"I am a good person who spends time trying to do the right thing. Although I have made many mistakes in my life, I have tried not to capitalize on them. I wouldn't consider myself a religious person, but I do believe in God. I have lived in several neighborhoods throughout my nineteen years on this earth. I now live on the south side of Chicago with my godmother, Mrs. Peterson.

"I have had many dreams during my lifetime, but my passion is law. I plan on attending Southern Illinois University this fall. My goal is to finish undergraduate school in four years. After I get my degree, I plan on attending law school. There are ten top law schools in the country and I plan on being accepted at one of them. It is kind of amazing that just four years ago, this dream seemed far out of reach. With hard work and dedication I have put into my studies this dream is now closer to reality.

"I know that the goals that I have set for myself will take a lot of commitment; therefore, I have to start today in order to accomplish my dreams for tomorrow. I will need the support of my family and close friends in order to make it through the tough times that lie ahead. The people that surround me will have to be wise and intelligent. My godmother has always said to me that 'The company you keep determines how far you go in life.' Also she has stated that 'It is not what you know but who you know.' I will always abide by these principles and continue to follow them throughout my life.

"If I could live my life over again, I would try to stay more focused on the things that matter the most to me. I would try to treat the people who helped me with the same kindness and concern that they showed me. I would work harder than I did in the past to excel. One thing I wouldn't change was the situation that forced me into the Child Welfare System as a 'ward of the state.' I have learned, experienced and overcome many obstacles that have not only made me a better person, but a more efficient decision maker. And I have turned mistakes into milestones of opportunity."

After reading Jason's entire story, I was impressed that someone so young could put all of his life's experiences into such perspective. One segment of his story entitled "Suddenly I Became Me" was indeed a revelation, a personal testament to the challenges that led to his growth and development.

When Jason left for college I knew that I wouldn't have missed the opportunity to be his guardian for anything in the world. It has been a priceless experience. We had forged a path through public and private schools. We had grown through teacher and student, then parent and child partnerships. We had suffered through crises, calamities, deaths and countless pains and problems. Yet we persevered and I have come to appreciate the depth of Jason's character, his resilient nature and his innate desire to succeed.

It has been an enormously gratifying journey.

Epilogue

Both Jason and Kevin have become the adults that any parent would admire. Jason is serving in the United States Air Force where he intends to complete his college education and perhaps go on to law school.

Kevin finished two years of college and is a successful real estate agent and home owner. He married a registered nurse and they have two beautiful children.

The relationship between the brothers is very close and each admires the other's accomplishments. I am extremely proud of the directions they have chosen and of their determination to do well.